TIP OF THE SPEAR

TIP OF THE SPEAR

An Intimate Account of
1 Canadian Parachute Battalion,
1942-1945

A Pictorial History

Lieutenant-Colonel Bernd Horn and Michel Wyczynski

THE DUNDURN GROUP
TORONTO · OXFORD

Copy-editor: Irene Karasavidis
Designer: Jennifer Scott
Printer: University of Toronto Press

National Library of Canada Cataloguing in Publication Data

Horn, Bernd, 1959–
    Tip of the spear: an intimate account of 1 Canadian Parachute Battalion, 1942–1945: a pictorial history

Includes bibliographical references.
ISBN 1-55002-388-8

1. Canada. Canadian Army. Canadian Parachute Battalion, 1st — History.
2. World War, 1939–1945 — Regimental histories — Canada.
I. Wyczynski, Michel, 1953– II. Title.

D792.C2H67 2002   940.54'1271   C2002-901092-6

1   2   3   4   5   06   05   04   03   02

THE CANADA COUNCIL | LE CONSEIL DES ARTS
FOR THE ARTS | DU CANADA
SINCE 1957 | DEPUIS 1957

Canada

ONTARIO ARTS COUNCIL
CONSEIL DES ARTS DE L'ONTARIO

We acknowledge the support of the **Canada Council for the Arts** and the **Ontario Arts Council** for our publishing program. We also acknowledge the financial support of the **Government of Canada** through the **Book Publishing Industry Development Program** and **The Association for the Export of Canadian Books**, and the **Government of Ontario** through the **Ontario Book Publishers Tax Credit** program.

Care has been taken to trace the ownership of copyright material used in this book. The author and the publisher welcome any information enabling them to rectify any references or credit in subsequent editions.

                                        J. Kirk Howard, President

Printed and bound in Canada.
Printed on recycled paper.

www.dundurn.com

Dundurn Press
8 Market Street
Suite 200
Toronto, Ontario, Canada
M5E 1M6

Dundurn Press
73 Lime Walk
Headington, Oxford,
England
OX3 7AD

Dundurn Press
2250 Military Road
Tonawanda NY
U.S.A. 14150

TABLE OF CONTENTS

AUTHORS' PREFACE

When Germany unleashed its offensive in Western Europe on 10 May 1940, it caught the world by surprise in many different ways. Specifically, the speed, efficiency and operational boldness of the new German doctrine shocked the Allies who were completely unprepared. Quite simply, Blitzkrieg introduced the West to an entirely new concept of war, one which was altogether different from that experienced twenty years prior.

A key component of Blitzkrieg, and one that astonished both the public and the military at large because of their feats of daring and martial prowess, was the German *Fallschirmjäger*. These intrepid troops very quickly became the epitome of the modern combat soldier. They introduced the third element, namely vertical envelopment. These German paratroopers were young, fit and audacious. They entered battle by way of parachute and were perceived as invincible. Europe was gripped by a sense of fear and paranoia. Fallschirmjäger were seen everywhere! Even the inimical British Prime Minister Winston Churchill, in that foreboding summer of 1940, feared an imminent German invasion spearheaded by 30,000 *Fallschirmjäger*. Simply put, paratroopers became the embodiment of modern war, the embodiment of offensive action and indomitable spirit. Not surprisingly, airborne forces soon became perceived by military commanders, as well as the public, as an integral part of a modern army. Although slow off the mark, by 1943, Britain and the United States developed airborne forces of unprecedented scale.

Canada was no different despite its hesitant start. It too developed airborne forces. Its effort, namely 1 Canadian Parachute Battalion, is the subject of this work. This book is a companion to *Paratroopers versus the Reich: 1 Canadian Parachute Battalion at War, 1942–1945*. Whereas the latter forms the scholarly examination of the Battalion, this book provides an intimate portrait in photographs of the unit's human side. Its title, *Tip of the Spear*, is derived from the first Commanding Officer, Lieutenant-Colonel G.F.P. Bradbrooke's explanation in 1942, that the unit was the "tip of the spear," and that its purpose was "to go in first, to penetrate behind enemy lines and to fight in isolated positions."

In sum, this book opens a window on the Canadian paratroopers both in preparation for, and in, battle. It comprises of approximately 450 photographs, most never before published. In its entirety, it is a visual record that captures the essence of the Battalion from its inception in July 1942 to its disbandment in September 1945. In these pages you will be able to follow the Battalion, more specifically, the individuals that provided the unit with its intemperate energy and radiant pride. The reader will be able to see in the young faces the unconquerable spirit of the paratrooper, as well as their dedication, unrivaled physical fitness and tenacity which made 1 Canadian Parachute Battalion the elite that it was. Without question, the Battalion, or more accurately its members, laid the foundation and established the airborne legacy that other Canadian airborne establishments could proudly follow and build on.

Although we have opted to utilize a pictorial format for this book, it is meticulously researched. Photographs and captions have been culled from both official and private sources. The National Archives of Canada, the National Library of Canada, the Department of National Defence Directorate of History and Heritage, the Canadian Airborne Forces Museum, and the 1 Canadian Parachute Battalion Association Archives were all carefully mined for both visual and textual records. In addition, the Public Record Office and the Imperial War Museum in London, as well as the Parachute Regiment and Airborne Forces Museum in Aldershot, England were also consulted.

This book is intended as a tribute to those adventurous souls who answered their nation's call to not only serve under arms, but to do so in an entirely new, dangerous and untested method of warfare. Quite simply, it is dedicated to the paratroopers of 1 Canadian Parachute Battalion. It is also our hope that this book will provide a lasting memory of their efforts, accomplishments and sacrifice.

FOREWORD

Very few of us, I believe, actually knew what we had volunteered for back in those dark days of the Second World War when we signed up to become paratroopers. Certainly, the young men of our generation, although cognizant of the horrors of the Great War, still felt that going to war for one's country was glorious and quite frankly, the honourable thing to do. Notwithstanding that, each of us had our own motives as well, whether it was the call of the unknown, the sense of adventure, the desire to be part of something new and untried, or simply the desire to have a crack at "Jerry."

Similarly, I doubt that many of us suspected that the unit we had joined, namely 1 Canadian Parachute Battalion, would become such an integral part of our lives, if not our souls. The friendship and camaraderie forged through the test of training and gruelling exercises, and consummated in the ordeal of fire on those bloody European battlefields, have made us a "band of brothers" that time will never change.

To turn these pages is for me, a leap back in time. To see the familiar young faces brings back a myriad of memories: soldiers ever so smart on parade, the bustle of our base camp at Carter Barracks, the commands echoing on the parade square. With every turn of the page I relive the marches along the English roads, the runs across fields in the countryside and the crack of the canopy as it opens. As I reminisce, I recall the unforgiving and unrelenting pace of activity and standard of performance expected of us. But as I am sure we all came to understand, this was absolutely primordial. The paratrooper's battle is unlike that of others — often isolation and a requirement to conduct operations unsupported for a period of time necessitates particular attributes in the individual airborne soldier. These qualities — fitness, initiative, tenacity and an unconquerable spirit — can only be fashioned through severely demanding training.

The net result of our training and ordeals was of course an unrivaled unit cohesion and combat effectiveness. But it was also an indescribable pride in belonging to something magnificent. I vividly recall the pride we all felt as members of the Battalion. It was plain to see whenever we had the opportunity to enjoy some leave: the sharpness of dress, boots that shone like mirrors and the manner in which individuals carried themselves.

This book, a compilation of hundreds of photographs and anecdotes from the veterans of the Battalion itself provides a graphic record of our efforts and achievements. It includes numerous photographs never before published. These have been painstakingly retrieved from the vaults of the National Archives of Canada, or have been rediscovered in the personal archives of the surviving Battalion veterans. The accompanying anecdotes and captions are often the actual words of the veterans who lived the adventure. Who can do better than this!

I wish to thank Lieutenant-Colonel Bernd Horn and Michel Wyczynski for their efforts in bringing this book to life. Their continuing commitment to the preservation and accurate documentation and dissemination of the Canadian airborne heritage is greatly appreciated. It is through efforts such as this that 1 Canadian Parachute Battalion's place in Canadian military history will remain prominently remembered.

Jan de Vries
President, 1 Canadian Parachute Battalion Association

Jan de Vries, President of the
1 Canadian Parachute Battalion
Association, 2000.

Private Jan de Vries, 1942.

BATTALION COMMANDER'S INTRODUCTION
(LIEUTENANT-COLONEL FRASER EADIE)

It has been almost sixty years since Canada first embarked on its unforeseen foray into the world of airborne forces. In those chaotic and dark days of World War II, our government, military commanders, and citizens regarded paratroopers as the cutting edge of a modern offensive army. We were also seen as adventurous and courageous, if not foolhardy, men prepared to enter a new and mysterious dimension of warfare that very few actually even understood.

However one describes the airborne soldier, he was, remains, and always will be, different. Those of us who answered the call of the Jumpmaster during the war years should be rightfully proud of our exclusive membership and accomplishments as part of 1 Canadian Parachute Battalion. We were specially selected through an unparalleled and rigorous selection process that ensured that only the very committed would earn the right to wear the coveted Jump Wings that denoted paratroop status.

Our trial of endurance and perseverance was continual as it was conceived to weed out those who proved to be incapable or unwilling to hold up to the physical and psychological rigours of airborne soldiering. Those few intrepid souls who successfully completed the gruelling training and then put it into effect in combat, laid the foundation of the nation's airborne legacy. Our unrivalled adaptability, initiative, physical fitness, and tenacity constituted the essence of our airborne spirit and set us apart from the others.

This distinction, however, did not come easily. It was earned through blood, sacrifice, and toil. During training the continual weeding out process never ceased. As paratroopers, we were always challenged and pushed. We were forced to either adapt and persevere, or perish. And adapt we did!

The Canadian paratrooper adapted to the American way of doing things in the stifling heat and dust of Fort Benning, Georgia. He adapted to the dust and high winds of the Manitoba prairie, in Camp Shilo, Manitoba. He also adapted to the Battalion's insertion into an entirely different army, namely the inclusion as part of 3 Parachute Brigade, 6 British Airborne Division under the command of the incomparable Brigadier James Hill. Among other things, the Canadian paratrooper was required to adapt to the change and training in the use of the British single parachute pack instead of the American two parachute T-5 assembly. This ability to adapt to change and quickly overcome all types of adversity became our Battalion's trademark. In the end, it is part of the reason we were able to do what we did under adverse conditions.

And adverse conditions they were! As paratroopers, we represented the sharp end. Brigadier Hill always enjoyed our unbridled spirit, or as he put it, our "*joie de vivre.*" We were always ready for a challenge — to have a go at it. For this reason he used us, as his "Cavalry." We always felt great pride in being chosen to do certain jobs; it provided great incentive to do better than the others. I think it is fair to say that we all felt a need to measure up; after all, initially we were strangers in a British brigade and division.

I clearly remember being summoned by Brigadier Hill during the break-out phase in Germany. He informed me that the Americans had failed to take Minden after several days of hard fighting. He now turned to his Canadians to finish the job. I asked him if we were to receive any support, and he replied, "No! That's why I'm sending you." He had great faith in the battalion and we never let him down.

Throughout the bloody battles in Europe, it was the courage and tenacity of the individual troopers who got the job done. There were never enough decorations to go around and never enough praise for the men who made each victory possible. But let me make one point clear — it was the individual paratroopers who forced their way into France on D-Day, helped hold the line in the Ardennes and Holland in December 1944 through February 1945, who jumped into a hornet's nest during the crossing of the Rhine in March 1945, and who clawed their way across the decaying but still dangerous Reich, who deserve the lion's share of the credit.

This pictorial history of 1 Canadian Parachute Battalion is but a small tribute to them. The authors have admirably captured the essence of the unit, both in spirit and accomplishments. In the pages that follow, I believe you will find a poignant reminder of the great things we achieved so many years ago. Needless to say, our proud legacy will live on in the annals of Canadian military history.

Lieutenant-Colonel Fraser Eadie, DSO, CD
Commanding Officer, 1 Canadian Parachute Battalion

1 CANADIAN PARACHUTE BATTALION AN OVERVIEW HISTORY

To say that Canada was unprepared for modern war in 1939 is not disputed. The Canadian Army numbered a scant 4,261 regular force personnel, with a further 51,000 Non-Permanent Active Militia members scattered across the nation. It was devoid of even the most rudimentary equipment, possessing only four anti-aircraft guns, five mortars, eighty-two Vickers medium machine guns, ten Bren guns and two light tanks. Needless to say, the idea of parachute troops was not even considered. In all fairness, in this respect Canada was no different than the British or Americans. Simply, very few nations, with the exception of the Russians and the Germans, invested energy or resources into the concept of airborne forces in the interwar years.

As a result, when the German Blitzkrieg sliced through the Low Countries and France in May 1940, the new face of warfare paralysed the Allies. One embodiment of modern warfare was the use of the German *Fallschirmjäger* (paratroopers). Overnight, Europe was gripped by an airborne paranoia. The spectre of airborne soldiers descending into hitherto safe areas was keenly felt clear across the English Channel. Even the combative and tough spirited British Prime Minister, Winston Churchill, anticipated a German invasion spearheaded by 30,000 German *Fallschirmjäger*. The parachute scare had a particular Canadian overtone. The expeditious withdrawal from the European continent under the pressure of the German juggernaut forced the abandonment of most of the British Expeditionary Force's equipment. As a result, the unbloodied Canadian troops found themselves the best equipped and organized to fight. Not surprisingly, they were now charged with the defence of the island. The need to defend against the airborne threat became one of their pre-eminent concerns.

The chaos and fear that the German paratroopers instilled was not lost on one Canadian staff officer who lived through the withdrawal of the Allied Expeditionary Force from Europe and the subsequent parachute scare in Britain. Colonel E.L.M. Burns quickly grasped the strategic value of the new airborne forces. To Burns, they exemplified a means of striking the enemy's command and logistical facilities located behind the front lines, thus, dislocating psychologically a belligerent's front line combat forces. Paratroopers, Burns realized, were a very potent offensive force that made the concept of a safe rear area obsolete.

Upon his return to Canada in July 1940, Burns immediately recommended the creation of a distinct parachute force for the Army. However, his repeated efforts failed. The Canadian senior military leadership saw no purpose for parachutists for the defence of Canada and especially not for an overseas role. The concept of "special troops" was alien and distasteful for a senior Canadian military leadership preoccupied with turning its long-neglected army into a modern organization capable of defeating the German war machine.

Of equal concern was the realization that these troops, because of the small numbers Canada could provide, as well as the operational role they would perform, would most likely be placed under British command. The issue of national command, which had its roots in the Boer War, and had been so hard fought for in World War I, was a very formidable concern and one that was not easily bypassed.

But, as in most cases with Canadian defence policy, the decisions of its Allies had a significant effect on Canadian thinking. As early as June 1940, Churchill demanded the establishment of a corps "of parachute troops on a scale of equal to five thousand." Churchill's direction was initially resisted as British commanders were more concerned with building up their savaged forces to defend England and eventually return to the Continent. However, the German invasion and subsequent seizure of the island of Crete, by *Fallschirmjäger*, in May of 1941, seemed to break the institutional resistance to parachute troops. By the spring of 1942, both the British and Americans fully embraced the concept of airborne forces. As the tide of the war began to swing in favour of the Allies, the focus quickly swung from one of defence to that of offensive. And nothing embodied offensive, aggressive action more than paratroopers! Not to be left out, senior Canadian military commanders quickly reversed their earlier reservations and recommended the establishment of a parachute battalion to J.L. Ralston, the Minister of National Defence.

The Minister's concurrence was quickly received and on 1 July 1942, the War Cabinet Committee approved the formation of a parachute battalion. Interestingly, the Committee specified that the purpose of this unit was home defence, specifically for the recapture of aerodromes or reinforcement of remote localities. Ironically, the inconsistency with the earlier estimates, as well as the changing tide of the war, was lost or seemingly ignored. Nonetheless, action to start-up the unit was quickly undertaken. That summer, eighty-five selected officers and non-commissioned officers (NCOs) serving overseas were sent to the Parachute Training School, Royal Air Force Station Ringway, in Cheshire, England. Similarly, in Canada, a group of twenty-seven intrepid volunteers under the command of Major H.D. Proctor deployed to Fort Benning, Georgia, in mid-August to commence American parachute training. In sum, these individuals became the first element of 1 Canadian Parachute Battalion. They would also form the initial training cadre to instruct the others.

Simultaneous with these developments, an effort was made to begin recruiting for the battalion at large. Messages were quickly sent to all Military Districts across Canada calling for volunteers to become paratroops. Furthermore, it was intended from the beginning, to develop a distinct Canadian program that combined the best of both the American and British parachute methodologies. Toward this end, on 25 July 1942 an Inter-Service Committee selected Camp Shilo, Manitoba, as the future site for the national parachute training centre. It was now only a question of time to erect the necessary facilities to support the training.

But a nation at war has no time to spare. Therefore, concurrently, and as an interim measure, National Defence Headquarters (NDHQ) reached an agreement with American authorities to send candidates to Fort Benning for parachute instruction. This allowed the ability to expeditiously commence training for the volunteers. It also provided the opportunity to conduct further research in terms of the type of facilities and special equipment required to set up the Canadian parachute training school in Shilo.

Although the Canadian airborne program had a slow, if not hesitant start, it now attempted to make up for lost time. A steady stream of candidates from across Canada poured in to the selection centres. On average, only 30 percent passed the initial screening process. Of these successful candidates another 30-35 percent would be lost during training. The demanding training regimen imposed on the few aspiring paratroopers that made it through the selection process quickly instilled in them the physical and psychological demands of this new type of warfare. First, it demanded an exceptionally high level of physical fitness. Second, it tested their personal courage and motivation every time they stepped up to the "door" to jump. It became quickly evident that not everyone was capable of becoming a paratrooper. Many would volunteer, but only a select few would earn their coveted jump wings. Notwithstanding the high wastage rate, the Canadian airborne program forged ahead.

In late September 1942, Lieutenant-Colonel G.F.P. Bradbrooke was appointed Commanding Officer of 1 Canadian Parachute Battalion. He was immediately faced with the imposing task of establishing a unit from scratch. The normal administrative and operational problems related to recruiting, locating and ordering the required equipment and weaponry, and preparing a challenging training syllabus were exacerbated by the fact that all this had to be done for an entirely new form of warfare that was not yet fully understood.

Adding to the difficulties of establishing the new unit was another dilemma. A second parachute unit, designated the 2 Canadian Parachute Battalion, had also been authorized in July 1942. The name of this unit, however, was misleading. It was not a parachute battalion, but rather a commando unit. The designation was assigned for security reasons to cover the true nature of its operational mandate. On 25 May 1943, this unit was re-designated the 1st Canadian Special Service Battalion. It represented the Canadian element of the joint U.S./Canadian First Special Service Force (FSSF). Its immediate priority on resources, including manpower, created a grave problem for 1 Canadian Parachute Battalion. NDHQ directed Bradbrooke to transfer all jump qualified personnel who volunteered to 2 Canadian Parachute Battalion. The rumour that 1 Canadian Parachute Battalion's supposed sister unit would see action before they would quickly circulated through the ranks. Not surprisingly, many of the aggressive and action-seeking paratroopers became frustrated with their Battalion's seemingly slow activation and transferred to 2 Canadian Parachute Battalion.

This latest problem added to the unit's growing pains. But Bradbrooke faced a yet more serious dilemma of retaining his qualified jumpers. Morale plummeted even further in the fall of 1942, when the senior military leadership determined that National Resources Mobilization Act (NRMA) personnel were entitled to join 1 Canadian Parachute Battalion. This infuriated the paratroopers. It was not lost on anyone that this implied that the Battalion would never see active duty overseas, because NRMA personnel were designated for Home Defence service only. Fortunately, this predicament was expeditiously corrected. Senior staff in Ottawa responsible for the establishment of the new parachute unit, along with the officers charged with its discipline and training, quickly advised the Chief of the General Staff (CGS) that the inclusion of NRMA personnel was sending the wrong message and as a result was causing serious recruiting and retention problems. The quandary was quickly rectified by announcing that "all parachute volunteers for the 1 Canadian Parachute Battalion must be active personnel." Simply put, all Home Defence personnel "were to be accepted only if they went active prior to their dispatch from their home district."

By end-December of 1942, most of the growing problems seemed to dissipate. A War Diary entry on 31 December reflected the growing optimism. "We feel confident," it recorded, "that the new year will see fulfilment of the original NDHQ plans and the Battalion will be distinguished when called into active combat overseas." The words appeared to be prophetic. The unit began to form a cohesiveness that subsequent calls for transfers to the First Special Service Force could not break. In addition, challenging training and a steady influx of equipment began to build a distinct sense of confidence and unit pride.

On 15 April 1943, the Battalion reported to its new home in Shilo, Manitoba. With the opening of the S-14 Canadian Parachute Training School, the Battalion could now meet all its training requirements in Canada. Nonetheless, the paratroopers were growing restless. They yearned for the test of battle. The young unit wanted the opportunity to prove its value. By the spring of 1943, Lieutenant-Colonel Bradbrooke, the Commanding Officer, publicly explained the role he and his soldiers were to play. "The paratroopers," he explained, "are the tip of the spear. They must expect to go in first, to penetrate behind enemy lines and to fight in isolated positions."

Not surprisingly, he tailored their training accordingly to ensure that his airborne troops would be prepared for their upcoming ordeal of battle. His focus was simple. It consisted of infantry battle-drills, weapons handling, parachute training, and physical fitness. Route marches became a dreaded component of the training plan. Demanding and gruelling training, which stressed psychological as well as physical strength, conferred on the paratroopers a sense that they were becoming different from the other members of the Canadian Army. Comparative to their infantry brethren, the airborne soldiers would have to operate on their own, often behind enemy lines with no secure rear area. The paratroopers would have to rely on their physical fitness, marksmanship, stealth and tenacity to hold their ground until the main force could link-up. The impact of the physically and mentally demanding training soon became evident. It forged a distinct identity for the airborne soldiers. It also gave life to a reputation for aggressiveness, courage and toughness.

While the training program raced on, the senior Canadian military leadership was left with the plight of determining what was to be done with the newly formed parachute unit. Clearly, a collection of aggressive and offensive-minded paratroopers would be wasted on Home Defence tasks, particularly as there was no threat to the Canadian land mass. Therefore, even before the paratroopers were considered operational ready, they were proffered up to the Commander of Home Forces in England. The British quickly accepted the offer, and in March 1943 stated that 1 Canadian Parachute Battalion would be included in the establishment of the second British airborne division that was forming. And so would begin a relatively short, but intense, relationship that would last to the present day.

Despite its aggressive spirit, the Battalion was not yet ready for combat. It had not completed collective training and even the most optimistic observers believed that it would require a further two months of preparation before being fully operational. Although reinforcements required to bring the Battalion up to strength were continually arriving from the now renamed A-35 Canadian Parachute Training Centre, there still remained a shortage of troops. This short fall, which would become more pronounced once the unit was involved in combat, as well as the specialized training requirement in regard to a paratroop unit, led NDHQ to establish a special Parachute Training company, with the specific mandate to train and provide qualified paratroopers as reinforcements for 1 Canadian Parachute Battalion. This sub-unit was later expanded to an entire battalion.

In late June 1943, the long wait was over. The Battalion's thirty-one officers and 548 other ranks deployed from Halifax, on board the Queen Elizabeth for overseas duty. The paratroopers subsequently disembarked at Greenock, Scotland on 28 July. On arrival, the unit discovered that it would be attached to the 3 Parachute Brigade, as part of the 6th Airborne Division. The Battalion rapidly settled into their quarters at Carter Barracks at Bulford Camp, Wiltshire and their training began in earnest once again.

Their new Brigade Commander, the incomparable Brigadier James Hill, was an experienced paratroop commander. He was the Commanding Officer of the British 1st Parachute Battalion and saw action in Tunisia during Operation Torch. While in North Africa, he was severely wounded and evacuated to England. Hill, based on his operational experience, believed that the gruelling nature of airborne warfare was such that the survival of his paratroopers depended to a great extent on their physical fitness. As such, he set demanding standards. For example, Hill expected a unit to cover fifty miles in eighteen hours with each soldier carrying a sixty pound rucksack and weapon. Ten mile marches within a two-hour time period were also considered the norm. In combination with fitness training, the initial two months in England also focussed on weapons handling and specialist training. Only once the foundation was laid did the Battalion and Brigade concentrate on collective training. The unit's outstanding performance and continual improvement was not lost on their brigade commander. During an exercise that simulated an invasion, in early February 1944, Brigadier Hill commented, "I feel I must write and congratulate you on the excellent show your battalion put up from the Albemarles on *Exercise Co-operation*. If they [1 Canadian Parachute Battalion] continue to make progress in this connection at this rate, they will soon be the best jumping exponents in our airborne corps and I should very much like to see them achieve this end for themselves. Well done."

The aim of the training was evident to all. Clearly, the moment to storm Adolf Hitler's *Festung Europa* was fast approaching. The planning and preparation for the invasion of Europe was now in the final stages. Missions had already been assigned. The 6th Airborne Division was responsible for protecting the left flank of the 3rd British Infantry Division which was to land on a beach west of Ouistreham. In turn, 3 Parachute Brigade was given the daunting tasks of destroying the coastal defence battery at Merville, demolishing the bridges over the River Dives in the area of Cabourg and Troarn, as well as controlling the high ridge centred on the small village of Le Mesnil that dominated the landing beaches. Moreover, the small village of Le Mesnil was a vital crossroads on the Cabourg-Caen highway and thus, critical for German efforts to manoeuvre in response to the invasion. The Brigade had the additional responsibility of harassing and disrupting the German lines of communication and defensive efforts to the greatest extent possible.

Brigadier Hill assigned 1 Canadian Parachute Battalion the responsibility of covering the left flank of the Brigade's drop zone (DZ) and protecting its movements within the DZ. The Battalion was also given three primary missions to be carried out in the eastern and central areas of the Robehomme-Varaville-Le Mesnil sector. "A" Company was responsible for the defence and protection of the left flank of the 9 Parachute Battalion in its approach, march, and attack on the Merville battery. "B" Company, and one section of the Parachute Engineer Squadron, were tasked to blow up two bridges spanning the River Dives. "C" Company, following its pathfinder assignment, was given the supplementary mission of destroying a German headquarters and bridge, as well as neutralizing enemy positions at Varaville.

And so, at 2230 hours, on 5 June 1944, members of "C" Company, 1 Canadian Parachute Battalion emplaned in Albemarles and left from Harwell Airfield to commence the assault against Hitler's Fortress Europe. These paratroopers were part of the invasion Pathfinder element tasked to secure and prepare the DZs for the main airborne assault. The remainder of the Battalion proceeded to Down Ampney and emplaned in Douglas C-47 aircraft. Their turn soon came. They were in the air by 2300 hours. The nation's first paratroopers were about to write a new page in Canadian military history and commence what would become a proud airborne tradition.

The Battalion crossed the channel and jumped into France between 0030 hours and 0130 hours, 6 June 1944. The drops were badly scattered over a wide area as a result of the lack of navigational aids and the heavy dust and smoke, which drifted over the drop zones from the heavy bombing of nearby targets. Heavy enemy anti-aircraft fire prompted pilots to take evasive action, which only magnified the difficulty of delivering the paratroopers accurately onto their objectives. For example, on the first drop, only thirty of a possible 110 paratroopers of "C" Company landed on the DZ. The subsequent drops were no better. The second group, made up of the main body of the Battalion, was scattered over an area forty times greater than planned. To add to the problems, numerous weapons bags ripped open, scattering the unit's vital heavy machine guns, mortars and anti-tank weapons, thus, significantly reducing the firepower available to the airborne soldiers in the following days.

In the midst of the growing chaos, the physical and psychological toughness honed by careful training, showed its importance and value. The paratroopers, as individuals and a collective unit, not only persevered, but flourished despite the unexpected situations and set-backs. By the end of the day, the resiliency of the Canadian paratroopers enabled them to attain all their assigned objectives with less than 30 percent of the troops and equipment originally assigned to the tasks. Having completed their assigned missions, the surviving paratroopers grimly dug-in to hold that which they had fought so ferociously for. Despite heavy losses, the Battalion held off all German counter attacks until the eventual Allied break-out. By mid-August, the tide had finally turned and 1 Canadian Parachute Battalion, as part of 3 Parachute Brigade, for the first time since the Normandy drop, was back on the offensive. Commencing 16 August, and continuing for the next ten days, the unit participated in an advance and series of attacks against the German rearguard until finally being pulled from the line. On 4 September, the Battalion began its departure from France and returned to its adopted home in Bulford three days later.

Unquestionably, 1 Canadian Parachute Battalion distinguished itself in its first combat action. However, this came at great cost. During the three-month period between 6 June and 6 September 1944, the Battalion sustained heavy losses. Of the original 544 paratroops dropped, 83 were killed, 187 were wounded and 87 became prisoners of war.

The unit's return to England provided the opportunity to rebuild and prepare for the next mission. The Battalion's first priority was bringing itself back up to strength through the integration of reinforcements from the 1 Canadian Parachute Training Company. Concurrently, the Battalion's new Commanding Officer, Lieutenant-Colonel J. A. Nicklin, focussed on correcting the deficiencies and shortcomings experienced during the Normandy Campaign, specifically on those skills required for offensive operations. As a result, the new training plan emphasized weapons handling, physical fitness, rapid clearance of drop zones, the efficient execution of offensive and defensive battle drills, and street fighting.

Although the tide of the war had turned, the Germans still maintained a powerful punch. In mid-December 1944, they launched a surprise attack in the Ardennes, an action which has became commonly known as the "Battle of the Bulge." Allied commanders quickly cobbled together all available forces to counter the latest enemy thrust. As a result, on Christmas Day, elements of the 6th Airborne Division, which included 1 Canadian Parachute Battalion, sailed for Ostende, Belgium. The Battalion was deployed to a series of villages where it was required to prepare defensive positions and conduct active patrolling. Although, engagements with the enemy were limited to only minor encounters, 1 Canadian Parachute Battalion earned the distinction of having been the only Canadian combat unit to see action in the Ardennes.

Once the immediate crisis was over and the German advance stymied, the Battalion was moved to Holland. By 22 January 1945, 1 Canadian Parachute Battalion established a series of defensive positions on the west bank of the River Maas facing German troops who manned a network of well-fortified defensive positions, which were part of the vaunted Siegfried Line, on the opposite bank. In the span of the next two weeks, aggressive patrolling, to test the enemy's defensive positions ensured daily firefights and shelling. The Battalion's routine continued in this vein, until it was eventually relieved in mid-February 1944 by American forces. So ended, the unit's second excursion to Europe, void of any major combat engagements. The Canadian paratroopers returned to Carter Barracks in England on 25 February 1945 to await its destiny.

Back in Britain, the Battalion began to prepare for what would become their final mission. In what is always a significant indicator, the Battalion was brought up to full strength. In addition, a tough training schedule was once again established. However, its duration was very short. On 19 March 1945, the paratroopers were confined to barracks. Not surprisingly, the air was heavy with anticipation and morale was high. Preparations, for what was to be their last airborne assignment, were in their final stages. The Allies were now ready to pierce the Reich itself.

1 Canadian Parachute Battalion's role in this historic event was under the umbrella of *Operation Varsity*, the designation for the airborne assault, as part of the crossing of the Rhine River, by the 17th U.S. and British 6th Airborne divisions, approximately five miles north-northwest of Wesel.

The paratroopers would once again be dropped behind enemy lines to seize vital ground, hinder enemy reinforcements and disrupt the German lines of communications. However, this time the drop would not supersede the main assault, but follow it. Senior military planners believed that greater use of firepower could be made to support the ground assault across the Rhine, if the artillery and air support were not impeded by paratroopers dropping in the target area. The necessity of accurate insertion onto the drop zones also led commanders to decide on a daytime jump.

Within this framework, 3 Parachute Brigade was assigned the task of seizing and clearing the "*Schnappenburg* feature" and the surrounding Diersfordter Forest. Once again, Brigadier Hill stressed the importance of "speed and initiative on the part of all ranks." Moreover, he directed that "risks will be taken, and the enemy will be attacked and destroyed wherever he is found." 1 Canadian Parachute Battalion was given the task of seizing the Hingendahlshof farm on the western edge of the drop zone and capturing the village of Bergerfurth, which was located south of the DZ. Within the larger framework, the Battalion was responsible for securing the central area of the Brigade's front encompassing wooded areas near a road linking Wesel to Emmerich.

The final drama began to unfold in the early evening of 23 March 1945. The Battalion's personnel emplaned in 35 C-47 Dakotas and shortly before 1000 hours the following day, the first of 14,000 troops, delivered by a total of 1,700 aircraft and 1,300 gliders, pierced the frontier of the Reich. The Brigade, consisting of 2,200 men, dropped in a span of only six minutes, with incredible accuracy, in a clearing measuring only 1,000 by 800 yards. 1 Canadian Parachute Battalion jumped at 0955 hours and was met by stiff resistance. The entrenched Germans, recognizing the clearing as a potential drop zone poured fire into the assaulting paratroopers. Despite the fiery opposition, within thirty-five minutes of the drop, eighty-five percent of the Brigade had reported in. Moreover, the Battalion secured its objectives by 1130 hours, less than two hours from the time they jumped out of their aircraft.

The Battalion now dug in and repelled numerous counter attacks. But soon the issue of greatest concern was the large number of prisoners that were captured, at one point equalling the strength of the battalion. This quickly became a logistical problem as space for the confinement of prisoners was scarce and guards to secure them were at a premium. That evening the lead reconnaissance elements of the 15th Scottish Division moved through the battalion to continue the advance into Germany. In the aftermath of the battle, the cost was once again tallied. Among the dead was the unit's Commanding Officer, Lieutenant-Colonel Jeff Nicklin. As a result, Major Fraser Eadie took command.

It was now evident that Hitler's Third Reich was quickly crumbling. For the Battalion, the final advance through northwest Germany began on 26 March 1945. Field Marshal Montgomery issued a simple directive which set the subsequent pace of events. "This is the time to take risks and to go 'flat out,'" he declared, "if we reach the Elbe quickly, we win the war." However, Winston Churchill was more forthright. He personally directed the British forces to beat the Russians to the Baltic Sea. What followed next was an aggressive six-week, 300 mile dash that ended at Wismar, on the Baltic Sea. There on 2 May 1945, the Battalion met the Russians, the only Canadians to do so.

The war was officially declared over on 8 May 1945. Later that month the Canadian paratroopers returned to Bulford, England and impatiently settled into Carter Barracks to await their future. Fortuitously, for the paratroopers, space was available on the Isle de France and the Battalion embarked for Canada on 31 May 1945. It arrived in Halifax on 21 June, the first complete Canadian unit to be repatriated. Lieutenant-Colonel Fraser Eadie, the Commanding Officer, received the Key to the City and a flag of Nova Scotia. Following a parade, the paratroopers were given thirty days leave and the individual paratroopers dispersed to the various parts of the country. The Battalion's personnel reassembled at Camp Niagara-on-the-

Lake, Ontario, in late July where it remained a unit on the War Establishment only as administrative tool. Unit members were offered the choice of discharge or service in the Far East, but as part of a different unit. The eventual capitulation of Japan, in August 1945, rendered the latter offer moot.

On 30 September 1945, 1 Canadian Parachute Battalion was officially disbanded. The nation's first airborne soldiers had earned a proud and remarkable reputation. Their legacy would become the standard of excellence that would challenge Canada's future paratroopers and imbue them with a special pride. The Battalion never failed to complete an assigned mission, nor did it ever lose or surrender an objective once taken. The Canadian paratroopers were among the first Allied soldiers to have landed in occupied Europe, the only Canadians to have participated in the "Battle of the Bulge" in the Ardennes, and by the end of the war had advanced deeper into Germany than any other Canadian unit. "The Battalion," wrote Field-Marshall Sir Allan Brooke, Chief of the Imperial General Staff, "played a vital part in the heavy fighting which followed their descent onto French soil on 6 June 1944, during the subsequent critical days and in the pursuit to the Seine. Finally, it played a great part in the lightening pursuit of the German Army right up the shores of the Baltic. It can indeed be proud of its record." Unquestionably, the paratroopers of 1 Canadian Parachute Battalion, as well as their supporting airborne organizations, the 1 Canadian Parachute Training Company/Battalion and the A-35 Canadian Parachute Training Centre, established, at great cost and personal sacrifice, the foundation of the Canadian airborne experience.

PART I

BEGINNINGS

The authority to form the 1 Canadian Parachute Battalion was given by the War Cabinet on 1 July 1942. The call for volunteers was promulgated shortly thereafter. In early August 1942, Brigadier E.G. Weeks, Deputy Chief of the General Staff, announced that the Dominion's aim was "to develop such a hard striking unit that it would have an efficiency excelled by no other such group in the world."

Courtesy of the 1 Canadian Parachute Battalion Association Archives.

Photographer Malak, National Archives of Canada, PA 209393.

"Three officers and 10 men are action-hungry and impatient to fill their role as the sharp, hardened tip of the Canadian army's 'dagger pointed at the head of Berlin.' The army picked them out of thousands of fit young Canadian soldiers who sought berths in the Canadian army's newest and already its elite corps, the first parachute battalion." Their Commanding Officer, Major H.D. Proctor, stated that their operational mandate would mean that they would "tackle jobs like capturing bridges defended or about to be blown up by the enemy or capturing headquarters behind enemy lines.... They must be prepared to do any jobs that cannot be done any other way."

Initially, a group of 27 officers and men were selected in Canada to undertake training at Fort Benning, Georgia, U.S.A. These individuals would then form the instructional cadre to train the remainder of the Battalion as it was established. Brigadier Weeks underlined that "the Department of National Defence feels that the last war has proven Canadian officers and men have the experience, guts and initiative and that the Canadian paratroopers will be second to none."

Photographer unknown, National Archives of Canada, PA 189754.

Photographer Malak, National Archives of Canada, PA 209387.

For the Allies, airborne warfare was still in its infancy. However, there was a realization that an emphasis on physical fitness was key. A Directorate of Military Training (DMT) report observed, "due to the fact that this type of work requires unusual stamina and mental attitude by personnel, parachute battalions must be considered as elite units. Therefore, in the early formative period of such a corps, volunteers should be selected who by reason of physical and mental standards and previous Military training are most likely to be able to succeed in this unnatural and difficult work."

Here aspiring paratroopers from the first group of 27 train prior to their deployment to Fort Benning.

Photographer unknown, National Archives of Canada, National Archives of Canada, PA 209711.

The Minister of Defence, Colonel (retired) J.L. Ralston inspected the initial group in Lansdowne Park Barracks, Ottawa, Ontario, prior to their departure. "It is a great satisfaction to us," he stated, "the way the men in the Canadian Army snap to it when there is a job to be done.... You are going at a time when things are a bit blue, when we are challenged to do everything possible and let out the last link in order to win this war. I know that you men are ready to let out the last link." Ralston finished off his address by imploring the intrepid individuals to "Bring back everything you can in the way of training, information and experience, so that this first parachute battalion will be the best that Canada can produce. If it is that it will be second to none in the world."

The Minister of Defence confers with Major H.D. Proctor, the officer selected by the Canadian General Staff as "the man most suited to lead the new force, which demands the utmost in resourcefulness and acceptance of risks even beyond those of other branches of the Service."

Photographer unknown, National Archives of Canada, PA 209712.

Major H.D. Proctor shares a moment with his officers.

Photographer Malak, National Archives of Canada, PA 209394.

Lieutenant-Colonel R.H. Keefler, from DMT, speaks with majors H.D. Proctor and R.F. Routh. Keefler was instrumental in the genesis of a Canadian airborne capability. In June 1942, he conducted a two-week visit to the American Parachute School, Airborne Command, in Fort Benning that resulted in a report that was pivotal for senior Canadian military leaders to understand the requirements of establishing a national parachute battalion.

Photographer Malak, National Archives of Canada, PA 209389.

Photographer Harry Rowed, National Archives of Canada, PA 209399.

The first group, according to their commanding officer, Major Proctor, were the "guiding lights of the future Canadian paratroops." Here Corporal N.R. Chapman undergoes Shock Harness training. This training mechanism was considered useful in determining whether an individual could become a parachutist. One parachute instructor later commented, "We can see his reaction to commands while he's in [the Shock Harness] and we can watch his facial expressions when he falls. It isn't unusual for a husky-voiced fellow to become a soprano."

The Shock Harness was one of the four training apparatuses attached to the High Tower. This training phase took place during the "C" Stage of the parachute course. Here, Corporal Chapman is being strapped into the harness in a horizontal position. When the harness was hoisted, the legs and feet would rise and the shoulders and head would dip towards the ground. The candidate would then be elevated to the top of the tower. Corporal Darrel Harris, a member of the first group of 27 candidates (who was later promoted Sergeant and appointed as a jumpmaster at the A-35 CPTC in Camp Shilo, Manitoba), still vividly recalled the shock harness initiation. He wrote, "Up he went, up and up, until the whim of the instructor was satisfied. It could be and usually was, right up to the top.... The rip-cord was dangling around on the right-hand side of the chest. On command, he was expected to grasp the rip-cord and give it a good firm yank. This action made the releases, then he plummeted towards the earth while counting 'one thousand, two thousand, three thousand.' At the same time he plummeted toward the earth [the individual] passed the rip-cord from his right hand to his left hand. This exercise was in place to keep one thinking while falling and counting. The 'three thousand' count was to be later used when jumping from the aircraft. If one didn't feel that mighty tug of the main chute opening by the time one had counted 'three thousand,' that meant there was likely some trouble brewing in the form of a malfunctioning main pack. So then the rip-cord was pulled and the reserve chute came into play."

Photographer Harry Rowed, National Archives of Canada, PA 205024.

BASIC PARACHUTIST COURSE — FORT BENNING, GEORGIA

The Basic Parachute Training Course given in Fort Benning, Georgia, was a physically and mentally demanding experience. All aspiring paratroopers who were dispatched to undertake the training were volunteers and had successfully passed a rigorous selection process. The four-week course was divided into four distinct stages as follows:

"A" Stage: Physical and endurance training, running, Jiu-jitsu and hand-to-hand combat classes.

"B" Stage: Instruction on ground landing techniques, landing swings, oscillation drills, exiting drills from dummy fuselages and Mock Towers, and wind machine training.

"C" Stage: Instruction on the various components of a parachute and their function, parachute packing classes, High Tower shock harness and controlled parachute descent training.

"D" Stage: Jump Stage. This was the climax of the course. Candidates put into practice everything they had learned to date. These included: administrative techniques of parachute retrieval from stores, the preparatory phases, in which the candidates adjusted and checked their main and reserves parachute assemblies prior to emplaning, emplaning and in-flight drills, preparing for jump and exiting aircraft drills, and landing and collapsing parachute drills. But most importantly, aspiring paratroopers had to successfully complete five daytime jumps to become parachute qualified. At any time during the training, a candidate could remove himself from the course. During "D" Stage, candidates who refused to jump were automatically failed and immediately returned to their units.

Controlled parachute descent training also took place during the "C" Stage. Two of the High Tower arms called "free arms" were used to practise parachute flight control drills. "On the free arms," explained Harris, "the student was hoisted to the top of the tower with the canopy of his parachute deployed and held in place at the apex of the chute by a cable. The skirt of the parachute was placed by fasteners on a huge metal ring that was the same circumference as the chute itself. Upon reaching the top of the tower, the mechanism automatically released the parachute and its human cargo, which floated freely back to earth as gently as, at times, a piece of thistledown. While it was a great deal of fun, it taught the student how to control the parachute whilst coming back down to terra firma."

Courtesy of the 1 Canadian Parachute Battalion Association Archives.

Photographer Harry Rowed, National Archives of Canada, PA 209411.

The airborne way — leading by example. Parachute training allowed no short-cuts or privileges for anyone, not even the commanding officers. Throughout the Basic Parachutists Course, officers and other ranks underwent the identical training and experienced the same hardships. This was one of the key reasons for the tight bond that developed between all paratroopers and is central to the airborne mystique. Colonel G.P. Howell, Commander of The Parachute School, Airborne Command, United States Army, offers words of encouragement.

Corporal Shaddock being lifted up the High Tower in Fort Benning, 15 September 1942.

Photographer Harry Rowed, National Archives of Canada, PA205021.

Photographer Harry Rowed, National Archives of Canada, PA205021.

Practising exits from a dummy fuselage. Even though this seems to be a simple procedure, the exercise encompassed a series of very important drills to assure proper exiting from the aircraft. For example, critical drills such as hooking up, verifying the static line, closing up to the door, positioning the body in the door frame, and exiting in a crisp manner, were practised during this exercise.

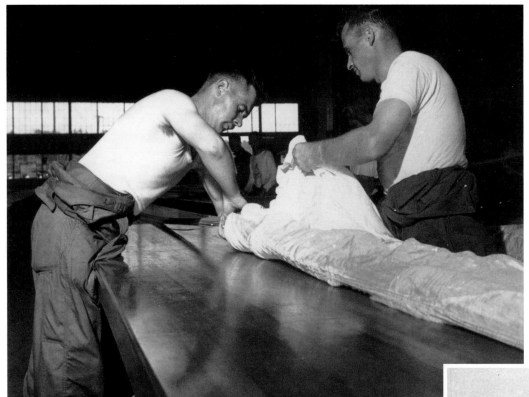

An important part of a paratrooper's training was the packing of parachutes. All Canadian parachute candidates sent to Fort Benning were required to undergo this training phase, which was conducted in the parachute hangars at Lawson Field. "You can rest assured," wrote Darrel Harris "that very close attention was paid to every detail. Our lives could depend on the job being well done." This component of training was deemed so important that it was included on the qualification certificate. For example, Harris's U.S. Jump Certificate read as follows: "This is to certify that: Corporal Darrel L. Harris (1st CPB) M-11204 has satisfactorily completed the prescribed course in Parachute Packing, Ground Training, and Jumping from a plane in flight. He is, therefore, entitled to be rated from this date, September 11, 1942, as a qualified Parachutist."

**THE PARACHUTE SCHOOL
AIRBORNE COMMAND**

Fort Benning, Georgia
1942

STUDENTS' TEXT

THE FOLLOWING TEXT IS TO BE USED IN CONNECTION WITH THE COURSE IN PARACHUTE PACKING. THIS IS THE ONLY TEXT TO BE ISSUED AND IT IS ESSENTIAL THAT EACH STUDENT KNOW THOROUGHLY THE INFORMATION CONTAINED HEREIN. DURING THE COURSE WRITTEN EXAMINATIONS WILL BE GIVEN ON THE SUBJECT MATTER CONTAINED IN THIS TEXT.

Photographer Harry Rowed, National Archives of Canada, PA 205017 and PA 209402.

Wind Machine training in Fort Benning, 15 September 1942. This contraption was utilized to simulate the difficulties of collapsing a parachute upon landing during windy conditions. It tested the candidates' strength and resiliency to quickly control, collapse, and extricate themselves from a parachute in the initial moments following the landing on a windy day. The machine consisted of a V8 engine attached to a seven-foot propeller, securely mounted on a truck chassis. A candidate would lie on his back in front of the machine, while forced air deployed his chute. When the canopy was opened, the wind machine was fully activated causing the billowing parachute to drag its human cargo unmercifully across the hard, jagged ground. The training objective was to stand up as quickly as possible to control and collapse the parachute.

Photographer Harry Rowed, National Archives of Canada, PA 209410.

Photographer Harry Rowed, National Archives of Canada, PA 209397.

The moment of truth. Canada's first paratroopers prepare to undertake their final test — an actual parachute descent. Each individual prepares for this trial in their own unique way. Nonetheless, the emotional strain is clearly etched on their faces.

One last dry run. Practising the exit drill prior to take-off. Note the extensive taping of the protruding door mechanisms on the fuselage to prevent hang-up or the accidental ripping, tearing, or cutting of the deployed static line.

Company Sergeant-Major A.T. Clifton ponders his upcoming parachute descent. The Riddell helmet he is wearing was ordered on a trial basis by the U.S. and Canadian Army, however it was found prone to severe cracking in cold weather and was, therefore, discontinued. It was replaced with the standard plastic liner for U.S. steel helmets with a modified chin strap.

One hour after this photograph was taken, Clifton described his first jump to journalist Winston Mills of the Evening Citizen. "If we took more than five seconds to make the jump, our instructor informed us it was a bad jump. It's a funny feeling when you plunge into space. They tell you down there that you will sweat it out as you fall — I can vouch for that — you certainly sweat. Once your parachute opens, however, you lose all sensation of falling and go into a sort of drifting, dreamy state. On the way down of course you yell at the other guys — they're quite close and you curse at some of them too, when they try to walk across the top of your chute. That's not funny."

Photographer Harry Rowed, National Archives of Canada, PA 209405.

Photographer Harry Rowed, National Archives of Canada, PA 209400.

Individuals are divided into sticks and await the order to load the C-47 Dakota transport aircraft.

Photographer Harry Rowed, National Archives of Canada, PA 209406.

Photographer Harry Rowed, National Archives of Canada, PA 209493.

Emplaning. The essence of parachuting was universal. General-Lieutenant Bruno Brauer, a member of the German Parachute Regiment and participant of the airborne invasion of the Low Countries in the spring of 1940, explained that parachuting "compresses into the space of seconds feelings of concentrated energy, tenseness and abandon; it alone demands a continual and unconditional readiness to risk one's life. Therefore the parachutist experiences the most exalted feelings of which human beings are capable, namely that of victory over one's self." Brauer concluded, "for us parachutists, the words of the poet, who said that unless you stake your life you will never win it, is no empty phrase."

Photographer Harry Rowed, National Archives of Canada, PA 205022.

Photographer Harry Rowed, National Archives of Canada, PA 205023.

An American Jumpmaster shares words with the aspiring Canadian paratroopers who Major Proctor described as the "instructors of the new (Canadian) shock troop unit."

American Jumpmaster checks the exit prior to a training jump, September 1942.

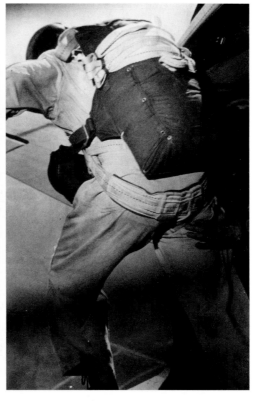

Courtesy of the 1 Canadian Parachute Battalion Association Archives.

Photographer Harry Rowed, National Archives of Canada, PA 209721.

And the tradition begins. Both the military and the public were mesmerized by the image of the fearless paratrooper jumping from the heavens. Major Proctor reinforced this perception when he explained, "Paratroops may be called upon to perform any job where it is difficult to get men to the spot by ordinary methods." Another Army spokesman added, "Keep your gun cocked, your knives ready, your eyes moving, and take to cover like a partridge, but do it silently. Remember you can't retreat!" The press quickly seized on the imagery. The Globe and Mail wrote, "Analyse that sentence! Picture men with muscles of iron dropping in parachutes, hanging precariously from slender ropes, braced for any kind of action, bullets whistling about them from below and above. They congregate or scatter. Some are shot. But the others go on with the job. Perhaps they're to dynamite an objective. Perhaps they're to infiltrate through enemy lines and bring about the disorder necessary to break up the foe's defence, whereupon their comrades out in front can break through. Or perhaps they're to do reconnoitering and get back the best way they can. But whatever they're sent out to do, they'll do it, these toughest men who ever wore khaki."

BEGINNINGS

The passing of a Canadian airborne pioneer. Major Proctor was killed in a freak accident on 7 September 1942, when as the first "jumper" during the inaugural parachute descent for the Canadian group, another aircraft severed his parachute lines. Corporal Harris recalled the terrible tragedy: "We had suffered a loss of a fine officer and gentleman," he stated with great emotion. "We had only known one another for a little over a month but our band had learned to respect each other to a high degree. The loss of our CO was not only bitter, it was devastating. Canada had lost a Commander and we, both officers and men, had not only lost our Commanding Officer, but a friend as well."

A fitting finale. The Canadian airborne cadre marches onto the tarmac for their "Wings" parade upon completion of their "Jump Course," on 12 September 1942, in Fort Benning. "It slowly dawned on us," observed one of the original Canadian parachute trainees, "that we were pioneers in our own way. The trail we were to follow might be a primitive one as far as airborne operations were concerned, but we had taken the first steps and now, we knew how to proceed."

The Canadian paratroopers are addressed by an American airborne officer prior to receiving their "Wings." The Canadians so impressed their American hosts that Brigadier-General Walter S. Fulton, Commanding General at Fort Benning declared, "It is thrilling to know that so fine a body of men is an ally of ours in this struggle against tyranny."

Photographer Harry Rowed, National Archives of Canada, PA 209401

Photographer Harry Rowed, National Archives of Canada, PA 208894.

Photographer Harry Rowed, National Archives of Canada, PA 198287.

Captain C.F. Hyndman, medical officer, receives his silver metal American "Jump Wings" from Colonel G.P. Howell, Commandant of the U.S. Army Parachute School. In regard to the experience, Hyndman stated, "Training has been hard and arduous ... we went through a series of toughening up exercises that would do credit to commando training.... It kept us on our toes all the time and at night we were too tired for anything other than a long sleep." He also described his state of mind as he was about to emplane the C-47 for his first qualification jump. "This is the moment, when stomachs behave in a quavering fashion, when knees deny the presence of bone and sinew, and when men's hearts come to a momentary pause."

Concurrent to the training in Fort Benning, on 24 August 1942, 85 officers and men, selected from the Canadian Army overseas, were sent to the RAF Parachute School at Ringway, Cheshire, UK for a two-week parachute course. They were identified as Course No. 24. Of the original group, 80 graduated on 8 September 1942 and were awarded their British Parachute Badge. An Army spokesman asserted that these individuals were "chosen for their mental and physical agility" and were to be "schooled in Britain in modern warfare's most dashing role — paratroops." Brigadier F. G. Weeks, Deputy Chief of the General Staff, rationalized dispatching troops to both Benning and Ringway. "Canada hopes to combine the best features of the U.S. and British paratroop technique," he told reporters, so that Canada would be capable of producing "the finest air-borne troops in the world." Only the best candidates would be chosen and those who showed signs of hesitation and doubt during

Photographer Captain Frank Royal, National Archives of Canada, PA 204956.

any training phase or exercise would immediately be stricken off strength. Weeks described what he expected from this new breed of tough and hardened warriors: "If a man even suggests he doesn't feel like jumping, he is at once removed from the battalion and returned to the unit from which he came. Any hesitation in wartime might spoil the entire operation."

COMPARATIVE PARACHUTE TRAINING—
THE AMERICAN AND BRITISH MODELS

When the first two groups of Canadian parachute-qualified volunteers returned from Fort Benning, Georgia, U.S. and The Parachute Training School, Ringway, Manchester, England in September 1942, they were ordered to undertake a comparative study of their respective parachute training courses. They were specifically directed to identify the best features of the two different training regimes and to use them to draft a distinct Canadian Parachute Training Syllabus. As the study progressed, the paratroopers were surprised at the large number of differences between the American and British programs. As a result of innovation and necessity, there was a dramatic divergence in both thought and practice. Nonetheless, it became evident that both countries had made, in a very short time, tremendous progress.

The Americans established The Parachute School, Airborne Command, United States Army in Fort Benning, Georgia on 15 May 1942. It soon developed into the major American airborne training centre of the Second World War, because it was more economical and practical to conduct all parachute training in one location. Aspiring candidates, regardless of rank, underwent a four-stage four-week course. Conversely, the British divided their parachute-training syllabus into two parts at separate training facilities. The first part, a one-week course, was held at Hardwick Hall, Chesterfield in Derbyshire. It encompassed preparatory selection and physical training. Successful candidates were then sent to The Parachute Training School, Royal Air Force Station Ringway, Manchester for the second half of their qualification training. During the following two weeks, the candidates underwent "synthetic" parachute ground training and completed the five required parachute descents from aircraft.

Between 1940 and 1942, the staff of these two parachute-training centres continually conducted numerous experiments, tests and trials to develop more effective and efficient ground jump training apparatuses that could accelerate the qualification of parachutists. The Americans made great use of various ground training equipment to simulate aircraft exit, canopy deployment, "in- flight" control, and landing drills. Two jump towers were also used. The 35-foot Mock Tower was designed to instil confidence in equipment and practise exits from an aircraft. Those who mastered their fear then progressed to the 250-foot High Tower. This intimidating structure was used for shock harness drills and for controlled parachute descent training. The shock harness drill was the toughest of all tower drills. Canadian parachute candidates dubbed it the "hangman's drop." The drill consisted of strapping a candidate in a special harness in a horizontal position with feet positioned higher than the head. As the aspiring paratrooper was raised, the body dipped into a forty-five degree angle with the head pointing towards the ground. In this very precarious position, the candidate was hoisted up the tower to a height ranging between 100 and 200 feet. Upon a given signal, the candidate pulled on a rip cord, which released him from the harness. The candidate dropped 15 feet and came to a violent stop designed to simulate the exit from an aircraft and the subsequent deployment of the canopy. The British also used a tower, theirs being only a 100 feet tall, to practice "in-flight" drills. They also used a wide variety of other types of ground training apparatus. Although different in design, their aim was similarly focused on exiting drills, canopy deployment, "in-flight" control, and landing techniques. However, the British preferred to conduct the initial descent training from an anchored static barrage balloon, elevated to a height of 700 feet, rather than from a tower structure.

Upon completion of their respective ground and descent training, the U.S. and U.K. candidates then prepared for their final training phase, the actual parachute descents. Under the American program, only five jumps from an aircraft were required to qualify. Upon completion, successful candidates were awarded the U.S. Army Parachutist Badge. The British course was more demanding. British candidates were required to complete two parachute descents from a static balloon, as well as another five jumps from an aircraft in order to qualify for their British Army Parachutist Badge.

Further differences were apparent in the aircraft that were used for qualification jumps and operations. Both used aircraft that were structurally distinct, and required different exiting and jumping techniques. The Americans adopted the C-47 Douglas Dakota transport airplane for their parachuting requirements. The paratroopers exited from a side door located on the fuselage's left side. The British opted for the Albemarle and the Armstrong-Whitmore Whitley converted bombers. The exiting procedure from these British aircraft consisted of jumping through a three-foot hole located in the fuselage's floor.

These very different exiting procedures also had distinct drills. The American Jumpmasters used a series of verbal commands and hand signals during training jumps. However, for operational and combat jumps, they relied on a two light system, activated by the pilot. The light box was located at eye level on the door's right side. Red meant that the aircraft was approaching the Drop Zone (DZ), and it prompted the Jumpmaster to initiate the exiting drill for the paratroopers, which was: Stand up, hook up and close-up to the door. When the green light came on, the Jumpmaster yelled "Go" and the paratroopers exited the airplane. Their British counterparts called Dispatchers also used a two-colour light system, which was also activated by the pilot. It was positioned above the hole, at eye level in front of the Dispatcher's position. When the red light came on, it confirmed that the plane was approaching the DZ and the jumpers immediately moved towards the exit hole. The first four paratroopers positioned themselves around the hole and the number one jumper placed his legs in it. When the green light was activated, the Dispatcher quickly ensured that each jumper was in the correct exit position before giving the 'Go' signal. During this time, he also used hand signal confirmations and verbal commands. Upon the given signal, the paratrooper executed his exit drill and waited for the static line to trigger the parachute's release mechanism. This was a stressful moment for the paratrooper who eagerly awaited the anticipated jolt that confirmed the opening and subsequent canopy deployment. The shock generated by the canopy's deployment was uncomfortable, but on a positive note, it meant that the parachute had been properly packed.

The packing of parachutes highlighted another departure point between the two countries. In the United States, the paratroopers were taught to pack their own parachutes. In England, parachute packing was initially part of the training syllabus, but this time-consuming responsibility was eventually removed from the training and conferred to the Women's Auxiliary Air Force, (WAAF). The Canadian experience was similar. Initially the packing of parachutes was adopted for training during the first months at the A-35 Canadian Parachute Training Centre. However, it was quickly stricken from the training syllabus and the packing, as well as certain repair tasks, were passed on to the Canadian Women's Army Corps (CWAC) personnel posted at Camp Shilo. The Canadian and English women performed their tasks admirably. In their respective packing areas, a large sign constantly reinforced the importance of their work, "Remember A Man's Life Depends On Every Parachute YOU PACK."

Further differences extended to the parachutes themselves. The Americans favoured a two-parachute system. The T-5 Parachute Assembly, comprised of a main parachute and a reserve worn on the paratrooper's mid-section. When the paratrooper exited the airplane, a fifteen foot static line, attached to the main parachute, triggered the release mechanism that deployed the canopy first. The British paratroopers were issued only one parachute, the "X" Type parachute. Its static line activated the release mechanism, but in this case, the suspension lines deployed first.

Because of the two-parachute system, the Americans preferred to drop their paratroopers from a higher altitude ranging between 1,200 to 1,500 feet. This allowed an individual extra time to activate the reserve if there were any technical difficulties with the main assembly. Conversely, the British chose to drop their paratroopers from 800 to 1,000 feet, citing tactical and safety reasons. A lower delivery altitude enabled the paratroopers to land quickly, thus reducing considerably the amount of time the paratrooper was at his most vulnerable; suspended in mid-flight. Clearly, in most cases, this low altitude negated the use of reserve parachutes, as there would be insufficient time to take action and too little altitude to activate the reserve. In addition, the staff at Ringway judged the two-parachute system to be too cumbersome and impractical, because of the limited three-foot exit hole in the floor of the Whitley aircraft.

The Canadian paratroopers preferred the U.S. parachute system, because of the reserve parachute safety feature. However, they favoured the British parachute harness quick-release box mechanism. This devise was located on the paratrooper's stomach area, and was activated by applying a pressing and turning motion. The mechanism disengaged the harness straps enabling the paratrooper to shed his harness in a matter of seconds. The American parachute harness was a more complex system, which involved tightening many straps located in different areas and took more time to remove. Both systems provided excellent support and could be adjusted to all body sizes.

Another dramatic departure point between the American and British practices was the actual drill for landing. The American method taught the candidates to land feet shoulder width apart. Due to the condition of the landing surface and the wind direction and speed, and rate of descent, the candidates were rarely, if ever, capable of landing with both legs simultaneously hitting the ground. Normally, one leg would hit first and, thus, absorb the entirety of the individuals body mass. Not surprisingly, American parachute school records confirm that many candidates suffered a variety of ankle, leg and knee injuries. The British method stressed the requirement to land with ankles, knees and legs held tightly together and slightly bent forward. In this manner, the lower body absorbed the body mass on impact. The paratrooper was also taught to execute a forward or side roll upon making contact with the ground to further assist with the distribution of the shock of landing. In the early fall of 1942, the British landing technique was evaluated by the Americans. It was subsequently incorporated into their own parachute training.

Even though the Canadians were late-comers to airborne warfare, having commenced their parachute training approximately eighteen months after their American and British counterparts, they proved to be quick learners. By October 1943, the Canadian paratroopers were the product of three different parachute courses. The 1 Canadian Parachute Battalion paratroopers underwent American parachute training in Fort Benning, Georgia from September 1942 to March 1943. When the S-14 CPTS (later A-35 CPTC) started its training activities in August 1943, all parachute candidates were trained using the new Canadian Parachute Training Syllabus. In July 1943, upon landing in England, the Battalion and all future Canadian parachute reinforcements were required to immediately undergo the British parachute conversion training. The American, British and Canadian parachute courses exposed the Canadian paratroopers to the best Allied parachute training available during the Second World War. But there was a real practical value to the different skill sets the Canadians were exposed to. The dual qualification greatly enhanced the Canadian paratroopers' operational value. It enabled Major-General Richard Gale, Commander of the 6 Airborne Division and Brigadier James Hill, Commander of the 3 Parachute Brigade, to utilize 1 Canadian Parachute Battalion in two important D-Day tasks in the early hours of 6 June 1944. The unique Canadian status of being qualified on both the British Albemarles and American C-47s aircraft gave their commanders the flexibility of dispatching the Canadians from the two types of aircraft, thus, ensuring the required force was available at the critical time to conduct the missions.

The varied experience also integrated the Canadian paratroopers into the airborne fraternity. In less than two years, 1 Canadian Parachute Battalion had developed into a formidable fighting force that earned its well-deserved place in the tightly knit Allied Airborne community.

Photographer Malak, National Archives of Canada, PA 209392.

Colonel Keefler addresses the graduating group of paratroopers just up from Fort Benning at Lansdowne Park Barracks, in September 1942. "Your real job is just starting now," he impressed on them. "You are the pioneers of this formation. You have to pass on the knowledge you have obtained to others. Naturally, there will be differences of opinion but I hope you will be open-minded. We want to use the best ideas of both the British and American systems."

Photographer Malak, National Archives of Canada, PA 209390.

Colonel Keefler examines the American Army Parachute Badge, commonly referred to by paratroopers as "Jump Wings," and congratulates Lance-Corporal W. Fitzsimmons on his accomplishment. Captain William P. Yarborough of the 501st Parachute Battalion, U.S. Army, designed this badge. It was formally approved on 10 March 1941. The badge was manufactured of oxidized silver 1 13/64 inches in height and 1 1/2 inches in width. It consisted of an open parachute on and over a pair of stylized wings deployed and curling toward the canopy. The Canadian Parachute Badge was still under design at the time.

"JUMP WINGS"

Throughout history, and regardless of nationality, badges and insignia have held a very special place in a soldier's heart. Nothing embodies this truth more than "Jump Wings." During the Second World War, a small number of Canadian paratroopers from 1 Canadian Parachute Battalion and 1 Canadian Special Service Battalion were given the opportunity to earn this badge of distinction. Circumstance and necessity meant that individuals would undergo one, or a combination of American, British or Canadian parachute training. Regardless, upon graduation, all successful candidates were issued with the highly revered "Jump Wings."

The American Army Parachute Badge was a silver plated metal badge. Located in the centre of the badge was an opened canopy with deployed shroud lines forming a "V". On either side of these converging lines were unfurled feathered wings, which curled up to the sides of the canopy. These badges were pinned over the left breast pocket of the Canadian Battle Dress or Service Dress Tunics. Canadian parachute candidates were authorized to wear these as of 11 September 1942. When the first Canadian Parachute Badges were issued in Fort Benning, Georgia, on 9 November 1942, an order was drafted shortly thereafter stating that Canadian paratroopers could no longer wear the U.S. Army Parachute Badge.

The British Army Parachute Badge was a cloth machine embroidered badge. A white deployed canopy was centred between two sky blue feathered wings on a khaki background. The badge was worn on the upper part (shoulder area) of the Battledress tunic's right arm sleeve. This badge was awarded to the first group of Canadian paratroopers who graduated from Ringway, on 8 September 1942. When the Canadian Parachute Badges were issued, the paratroopers who wore the British Army Parachute Badges were also ordered to remove them. Later, in 1943, certain groups of 1 Canadian Parachute Battalion paratroopers and parachute reinforcements, who successfully underwent British parachute conversion training, were given British Army Parachute Badges as souvenirs.

The Canadian Parachute Badge was a cloth machine embroidered badge. A white deployed canopy was centred between two horizontal wings. The shroud lines were placed behind a gold colour maple leaf. The badge was stitched onto a dark green backing. The badge was sewn over the left breast pocket of the Battle Dress and Service Dress tunics. It was also later worn on the paratroopers' Denison Jump Smocks.

Sergeant W. Tobin adjusts his new "jump" boots. These brown boots were the envy of most regular soldiers who were required to wear the standard black issue ankle boot with gaiters. The Benning group was the first Canadian paratrooper group to wear this type of footwear in the Canadian Army. "After five jumps," recalled Corporal Herb Peppard, "I was presented with my wings and issued a beautiful pair of brown jump-boots. They were high boots, unique to the Canadian Army. Before this, only officers had been permitted to wear brown shoes or boots. I spent a lot of spare time polishing these precious boots." Corporal Harris adds, "We were extremely proud of wearing those nice high-topped jumps boots. This may have been the first time in Canadian military history when NCOs and other ranks were allowed to wear brown boots since that privilege had been the domain of the Commissioned Officers. [To say that] we were proud of these boots would be something of an understatement."

Later, this new item of dress swayed Jan de Vries and numerous other young Canadians to volunteer for airborne service. "I recall," conceded Jan de Vries, "seeing a parachute recruiting officer wearing them. One look and that did it for me."

Photographer unknown, National Archives of Canada, PA 208630.

The Canadian Parachute Badge. The first sketches of this badge were drawn under the supervision of Major R.F. Routh and Colonel F. Duguid, Head of the Historical Section at NDHQ. The first Canadian "Wings" were issued to Canadian paratroopers training in Fort Benning, Georgia on 2 November 1942. This new insignia identified the wearer as a special breed of warrior and quickly became the envy of other military personnel. Regrettably, it did not take long for non-airborne personnel to obtain them through illicit means. They often pinned the unauthorized badge on and headed to the local bars and dance halls to impress the ladies. Measures were immediately taken to correct this situation. In early January 1943, all qualified parachutists were issued a Canadian Parachute Badge card that had to be carried by qualified personnel at all times. This card had to be presented upon request to confirm that the individual was in fact a qualified paratrooper. Non-qualified personnel caught wearing this badge faced disciplinary action.

PARACHUTISTS' SONG FROM THE PARACHUTE TRAINING SCHOOL AT RINGWAY

When first I came to P.T.S., My C.O., he advised

take lots and lots of underwear, you'll need it I surmise

But I replied "My God Sir, no matter what befall

I'll always keep my trousers clean when jumping

through the hole"

(Chorus)

Jumping through the hole, jumping through the hole

I'll always keep my trousers clean when jumping through the hole

I went into the hanger, instructor by my side,

and on "Kilkenny's Circus" had many a glorious ride

on these ingenious gadgets said he to one and all

will centralize your C of G when jumping

through the hole

(Chorus)

He swung me on the swings boys, he slid me down the slide

I saw the glorious static chute with camouflage design

I heard the Warrant Officer shout such a lovely line

"This lovely bit of stuff boys," said he upon my soul

"Is sweeter than your sweetheart when you're jumping

through the hole"

(Chorus)

One morning very early, cold and bleak and dark
They took me in a so-called bus, out to Tatton Park
They fitted me with parachute and helmet for my head
The sergeant looked with expert eye, "They fit you fine" he said
"But in keeping with the weather," I said to one and all
"I take a dim and misty view of jumping
through the hole"
(Chorus)

"OK, up seven hundred, five to drop" said he
"Five to drop, by God," I cried and one of them is me
and clinging very grimly to the handles on the floor
I cursed the day I volunteered for jumping through the hole
Then he bellowed "Action Stations" and he bellowed "Go"
Then I found I couldn't stop myself from jumping
through the hole
(Chorus)

I hit my pack, I rang the bell, I twisted twenty times
and came down with both feet entangled in my
rigging lines
But floating upside down to earth, I didn't care at all
For I kept my trousers clean when jumping
through the hole
(Chorus)

And now I've got a badge boys, of badges it's the best
I'm more proud of it than the hairs upon my chest

To all admiring men, it doth a mighty deep entoll

The keeping of the trousers clean when jumping

through the hole

(Chorus)

This song was sung to the music of an Irish song 'Rose of Trallee'

PART II

BUILDING A NATIONAL AIRBORNE CAPABILITY

The Battalion's instructor cadre, formed from the graduates of both Benning and Ringway, now came together to provide a distinctive Canadian parachute-training program. The training program was designed to accommodate monthly drafts of 50 individuals starting in October 1942.

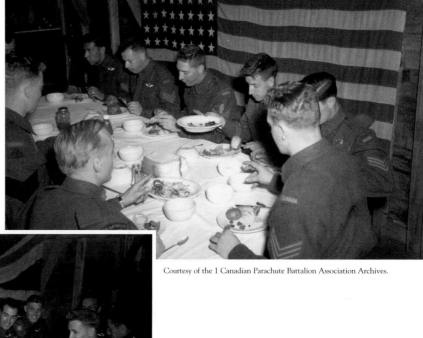

Courtesy of the 1 Canadian Parachute Battalion Association Archives.

Courtesy of the 1 Canadian Parachute Battalion Association Archives.

Although the intent was to establish a distinct Canadian parachute-training establishment, the urgent need for trained parachutists demanded co-operation with Canada's allies. Time was still needed to complete the S-14 Canadian Parachute Training School in Shilo, Manitoba and gather the necessary equipment. As a result, an agreement was reached with the Americans to utilize their facilities. One again, Canadian paratroopers and candidates made Fort Benning their temporary home.

Although stationed on a huge American base, and outfitted with U.S. equipment, an effort was still made to maintain a distinct Canadian identity. Brigadier James Hill aptly described the unique nature of the Battalion during the unveiling of a commemorative plaque in 1997. As their former Brigade Commander, he stated, "I could not help feeling in those far off days that I had been entrusted with — and had a great responsibility for — a magnificent body of fighting men, who were Canada's answer to Winston Churchill's stirring call in August 1940 for a great parachute force. The 9 Canadian Provinces — the Yukon, Newfoundland and the North West Territories, spanning together a distance of some 3,500 miles, were represented amongst their number, as were 156 French Canadians and 49 Canadian Indians. They were young, with an average age approaching 22, they were drawn from all walks of life."

The reality of wartime expansion: living quarters were rudimentary at best. "Billets had been arranged for us in the area of the base known as 'the Frying Pan,'" explained Corporal Harris. He added, "The huts were built with no foundation, being placed on posts and beams a foot or two above the ground. Tarpaper or light roofing paper adorned the outside up to about four feet. Wooden strapping held it in place." Boyd Anderson, a 1 Canadian Parachute Battalion recruit, came to Fort Benning in January 1943 and described the inside of these billets as follows: "In each hut there were single cots and a small wood burning stove. The weather was mild, even hot in the daytime, but at night, a cold dampness set in. Some of the nights at Fort Benning were as cold as any I ever put in. We only had thin blankets, so we shivered. If someone was able to scrounge a little wood, a fire was started. When it rained, which was often, water ran over the hardpan ground with a reddish color. It was said that the Georgia soil was red from the blood of the southern soldiers killed in the American Civil War."

Donald R. Burgett, an American parachute candidate who trained at Benning in spring 1943, provided an additional perspective on the quarters in the Frying Pan. "Small barracks stood in orderly rows behind weather-beaten tents. The barracks weren't painted, and there was no glass in the windows — just large wooden shutters jutting over the screened opening, to be let down in case of foul weather. These buildings were set up on short posts or footings; each had two steps up to a door opening set in the center of the front. Some of the dwellings even had doors on the door openings. Two rows of these barracks faced each other, forming a sort of street down the centre. At one end, the mess halls ran at right angles with the company street, forming a large 'T.' At the other end, and set apart from the company street, were the latrines; then farther down the hill, and closer to the blacktop road, was the P.X. and gambling equipment — one-armed bandits and all."

Although the nature of airborne warfare was still relatively unknown to the Allies, one thing was known for sure — the stamina required to undertake the training and physical hardship of parachuting, much less airborne operations, necessitated one underlying characteristic of the paratrooper — youth.

Courtesy of the 1 Canadian Parachute Battalion Association Archives.

Courtesy of the 1 Canadian Parachute Battalion Association Archives.

The Battalion's members represented the cream of the Canadian Army. The press reported that "They are good, possibly great soldiers, hard, keen, fast-thinking and eager for battle. They come from both coasts, from the prairies, the cities of Ontario, from the British Columbia lumber camps."

Pictured are: Corporal Chapman and Lance Corporal Wilton.

Nothing exemplified airborne training more than the physical fitness training. Dan Hartigan recalled that "they wore you down until you had nothing left and that it was during times like this that they offered you the opportunity to quit ... it was tough." Visiting media concurred. "The training is going to be so tough that some of the paratroops are expected to drop out," they reported, "worn to a frazzle by the hardest kind of gruelling work, even though they are hand-picked and have had full infantry training." Darrel Harris wrote, "I always felt there was a real sadistic streak which formed a part of the composition of these American instructors. They really gave it to us and I think they were doing the best to see to it that we caved in. We, however, had something to prove." Even though Canadian candidates thought they were treated harshly because of their nationality, their American counterparts were exposed to the same demanding tempo and gruelling exercises. Quite simply, it had nothing to do with being American or Canadian — it had everything to do with qualifying only the toughest and very best soldiers. Donald R. Burgett, an American parachute candidate, remembered a sergeant parachute instructor's welcome speech. "We're going to be tough," warned the PI, "on everyone here, and don't expect any sympathy from any of us any time, because we are going to do everything we can to make you quit the Paratroops."

Photographer Lieutenant S.E. Smith, National Archives of Canada, PA 209714

Courtesy of the 1 Canadian Parachute Battalion Association Archives.

Dr. George T. Stafford, Professor of Physical Education at the University of Illinois, was the inventor of the Trainasium, the Stafford Training Structure, which was a new physical fitness training device. It contained 22 exercise stations that thoroughly worked each muscle group. Certain stations focused on developing the candidates' sense of balance, as well as psychological ability to working in elevated and confined areas. The structure was built by the Potamac Engineering Service Company, tested by the U.S. Army, and adopted as a training tool at Fort Benning. During the research and construction of the apparatus, Stafford read William L. Shirer's *Berlin Diary: The Journal of a Foreign Correspondent, 1934–1941*. He was so impressed by an excerpt comparing the physical conditioning of British and German soldiers after the fall of Belgium that he included it in the Trainasium training manual, underling the fact that physical fitness would be an imperative training component of future armies. The cited passage read as follows:

"Returning from Brussels to Aachen, we ran across a batch of British prisoners. It was somewhere in the Dutch province of Limburg, a suburb, I think Maastricht. They were herded together in a brick-paved yard of a disused factory. We stopped and went over to talk to them. They were a sad sight. Prisoners always are, especially right after a battle. Some were obviously shell-shocked, some wounded and dead tired. But what impressed me most about them was their physique. They were sallow-chested and skinny and round-shouldered. About a third of them had bad eyes and wore glasses. Typical, I concluded, of the youth that England had neglected so criminally the twenty-two post-war years when Germany, despite its defeat and the inflation of six million unemployed, was raising its youth in the open air and the sun. I asked them where they were from and what they did at home. About half of them were from offices in Liverpool; the rest from offices in London. Their military training had begun nine months before, they said when the war started. But it had not, as you could see, made up for the bad diet, the lack of fresh air and sun and physical training, of the post-war years. Thirty yards away German Infantry were marching up the road

Courtesy of the 1 Canadian Parachute Battalion Association Archives.

towards the front and I could not help comparing them with these British lads. The Germans were bronzed, clean cut, physically healthy-looking as lions, chests developed and all. The English youngsters, I knew, had fought as bravely as men can. But bravery is not all; it is not enough in this machine-age war. You have to have a body that will stand terrific wear and tear. And then, especially in this war, you must have all the machines of warfare. I asked the English about that. There were six of them, standing a little apart — all that were left, they told me, from a company that had gone into battle near Louvain. 'We didn't have a chance,' one of them said. 'We were simply overwhelmed.' "

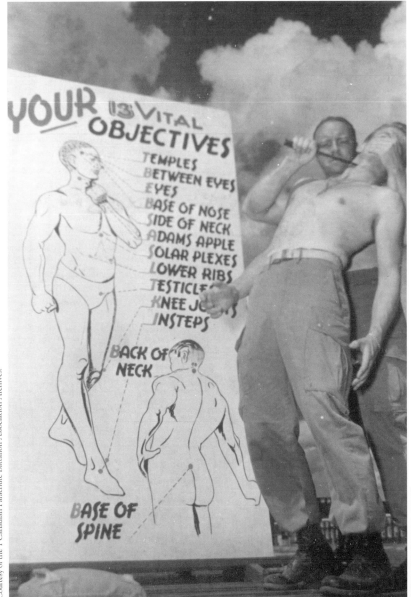

Unarmed combat was another central component of the paratrooper's training. Firstly, it was a function of developing aggressiveness and practical fighting skills. It was also designed to raise the individual's level of self-confidence.

Photographer Harry Rowed, National Archives of Canada, PA 209734.

A second component of unarmed combat was its physical aspect. It required endurance, strength, and simply toughness. Private E.W. Harrington felt that "Training was very rigorous, a real challenge. They put us through hell and high water. We were told if you can't stand the pace — get out now. This slowly weeded people out. It got rid of those marginal types." All parachute candidates had to undergo a series of Jiu-Jitsu self-defence courses. If a paratrooper ran out of ammunition, he was expected to use any means at his disposal to forge on and complete his task. His body was to be considered a lethal weapon. During a demonstration to the first group of volunteers, a black belt instructor in Jiu-Jitsu stated, "If you have to break his arm, break it. We'll fix him in the hospital."

Courtesy of the 1 Canadian Parachute Battalion Association Archives.

Photographer Lieutenant S.E. Smith, National Archives of Canada, PA 204980.

Courtesy of the 1 Canadian Parachute Battalion Association Archives.

Distinctive landmarks — the High Towers of Fort Benning. The High Towers in Fort Benning were built a few months after the organization of the U.S. Parachute Test Platoon in July 1940. Lieutenant-Colonel William C. Lee, a member of the staff of the Chief of Infantry, recommended that the paratroopers be sent to the Safe Parachute Company in Hightown, New Jersey to conduct training on parachute drop towers that had been built for the New York World's Fair. The assessments of the returning paratroopers in regard to these 250-foot towers were so positive that the Army immediately placed an order for the construction of two towers. A short time later, two others were built. During Lieutenant-Colonel Keefler's June 1942 visit at the Fort Benning Parachute School, he was given an overview of the High Towers' training capabilities, as well as demonstrations of controlled and free fall jumps, and shock harness training.

Keefler took numerous photographs during these demonstrations and was loaned a set of blueprints. Each tower contained approximately 60 tons of structural steel. A control hut was located inside the tower's base, where instructors could activate and control a series of electric driven winches, cable and pulley apparatuses, and parachute release devices. It was estimated that to build such a training device in Canada would cost approximately $50,000 dollars. A month after Keefler's return, Camp Shilo was selected as the future site for the Canadian Parachute Training School. When 1 Canadian Parachute Battalion relocated to Camp Shilo in April 1943, the Canadian High Tower, identical to those in Fort Benning, was fully operational.

Courtesy of the 1 Canadian Parachute Battalion Association Archives.

Courtesy of the 1 Canadian Parachute Battalion Association Archives

Although strength and toughness were a must, parachuting also depended on a sound understanding of jump drills and techniques. Various apparatuses were specifically developed to assist in practising the requisite parachuting skills. Platforms and landing swings were utilized to train individuals in the proper rolling technique on landing.

Photographer Lieutenant S.E. Smith, National Archives of Canada, PA 209713.

Flight Training was designed to teach candidates how to manoeuvre their canopies while in the air to avoid collisions with other jumpers and to try and avoid obstacles on the ground.

Photographer Lieutenant S.E. Smith, National Archives of Canada, PA 204979.

Courtesy of the 1 Canadian Parachute Battalion Association Archives.

Aircraft drills were practised in dummy fuselages and covered everything from boarding to finally exiting the aircraft.

The most dreaded of training apparatuses was the 35-foot Mock Tower. Amazingly, individuals found jumping from the Tower more intimidating than exiting from a real aircraft. One reporter noted, "Paratroop training is a series of can-you-take-it tests based on practical psychology." The relative infancy of the Allied airborne effort is evident from the not-yet-completed Mock Towers. Corporal Harris reminisced, "Then there was the 35-foot tower. Now 35 feet is not particularly high, but one gets a very distinct sense of height from there. On this unit, the victim put on the now familiar parachute harness after climbing up the ladder to the 35-foot mark. At this point, he would find a small room with an instructor. The whole thing was similar to the landing trainer, except that when the student jumped out, he fell about ten feet and then his fall was halted by a sloping cable connected from the tower to an elevated anchor on the ground. It served a very valuable purpose, in that it taught the student how to make a proper exit from the aircraft when the time came."

The Mock Tower was an imposing hurdle. Private J.A. Collins remembered, "'B' Stage was nicknamed the 'man breaker' for this stage had the highest number of failures." This impression was borne out by an official report. Lieutenant-Colonel W.B. Webb wrote, "the total average wastage in any class going through the school ranges about 25%, but 15% is due to accidents and 10% to refusals." These refusals, he added, "nearly all take place when the volunteer is faced with the apparatus [Mock Tower] from which he must throw himself into space."

Courtesy of the 1 Canadian Parachute Battalion Association Archives.

In Fort Benning the packing of parachutes was still a component of training. This, however, was later dropped from the Canadian Parachute Training Centre syllabus in Camp Shilo.

Courtesy of the 1 Canadian Parachute Battalion Association Archives.

1 Canadian Parachute Battalion members with mascot in Fort Benning.

Courtesy of the 1 Canadian Parachute Battalion Association Archives.

Courtesy of the 1 Canadian Parachute Battalion Association Archives.

Pre-jump drills — dressing, calling the roll, and checking equipment. The potential hazard of parachuting necessitated the strict adherence to detail.

The mystique and allure of parachuting drew many. Private Jeff Kelly recalled, "I heard about the paratroopers. They were the best. We heard about them and they were tops in the army. They were the only outfit that I wanted to get into. I just wanted to parachute and I knew that they were the best."

SELECTION REQUIREMENTS

The physically and mentally challenging nature of airborne warfare required the implementation of a very rigorous screening process that would allow only the finest candidates to be selected for further training. Army psychiatrists developed a rating system that was to grade volunteers during selection boards. This system ranked an individual from a range of "A" to "E", "A" representing the most preferred, and "E" representing the least desirable. Only those who achieved an "A" score were kept for airborne training. The Army psychiatrists were confident that the "A" candidates were the best Canada could offer. They were equally sure that those awarded an "E" rating should not be considered. However, there was a large degree of uncertainty in regards to the approximate 80% who fell into the grey area in-between.

The volunteers were expected to have an exceptionally high standard of mental, physical, and psychological fitness. The aspiring paratrooper was required to be in good physical condition, preferably with a history of participation in rugged sports or a civilian occupation demanding sustained exertion. Aggressiveness, emotional stability, high motivation, and self-reliance were also necessary prerequisites to achieve an "A" rating. The volunteer needed a minimum education of Grade 6, which was a higher standard than that required by the conventional Canadian infantry. Furthermore, at the start, all hopefuls had to be qualified Basic Training. This requirement was later dropped as a result of dwindling numbers of volunteers. Once training was underway, the Army psychiatrists were able to refine their selection procedures based on the performance of those who completed the requisite parachutist course and subsequent operations. The official "Medical Standards for Parachute Troops" are given below.

Medical Standards for Parachute Troops — All Ranks

A. Alert, active, supple, with firm muscles and sound limbs, capable of development into aggressive, individual fighter with GREAT endurance.

B. Age: 18–32 both inclusive.

C. Physically qualified as follows:

1. Weight: Maximum not to exceed 190 lbs.
2. Height: Maximum not to exceed 72 inches.
3. Vision: Distant vision uncorrected must be 20/40, each eye.
4. Feet and Lower Limbs: Flat feet not acceptable. Better than average bone structure and muscular devel opment of the lower limbs.
5. Genito-urinary System: Venereal disease to disqualify.
6. Nervous System: Evidence of highly labile nervous system to disqualify. History of nervous com plaints to disqualify.
7. Bones, Joints and Muscles: Lack of normal mobility in every joint, poor or unequally developed musculature, poor co-ordination, asthenic habitus, or lack of better than average athletic ability to dis qualify.
8. Hearing: W.V.-10ft. Both ears, i.e. a man standing with his back to the examiner and using both ears must be able to hear a forced whisper 10 ft. away. Must have patent Eustachian Tubes.
9. Dental: Men must not drop with false teeth; consequently there must be eight sound or reparable teeth (including 2 molars) in the upper jaw, in good functional opposition to corresponding teeth in lower jaw.
10. Medical History: A history of painful arches, recurrent knee or ankle injuries, recent or old fractures with deformity, pain or limitation of motion, recurrent dislocation, recent sever illness, operation or chronic disease to disqualify, (unless recurring, properly healed fractures not to disqualify).
11. Other than as listed above, physical standards to be the same as Army standard ₄ A.1.

D. Mentally qualified as follows:

1.a. Emotional instability and poor motivation are the two outstanding causes of failure. Signs of mild instability not sufficient to warrant lowering of category, may be sufficient to warrant rejection as paratroopers.

2. Physical signs: Rapid pulse, tremor of hands or face, sweating of the extremities, while not sufficient in themselves to warrant rejection are of real importance in conjunction with other signs of instability.

3. Psychiatric History: Direct questioning may be employed inasmuch as all of the soldiers examined are presumably anxious to become paratroopers. Childhood fears and phobias, night terrors, sleep walking, enurcsis since the age of 8, are important. Present fear of heights, water, or closed places to disqualify, as well as combinations of such symptoms as palpitation, nocturnal dyspnca, stomach disorders, frequent headaches, low back pains, and urinary frequency to disqualify.

4. Psychotic or psychopathic tendencies to disqualify.

5. The seclusive, lonely type of individual appears to do poorly with this unit.

6. Volunteers who are under stress due to circumstances at home are apt to fail, for example, those who have recently married or whose wives or parents have not given their consent for participation in paratroops training.

7. Should be of average intelligence with an "M" score not lower than 115.

8. It should be carefully determined that the candidate is anxious to become a paratrooper, and that he has full knowledge of what paratroop training entails.

Former Winnipeg Blue Bomber star, Major Jeff Nicklin, originally qualified in Ringway. He was now required to undertake his U.S. conversion training. Sergeant Andy Anderson believed that "Jeff Nicklin was one who almost seemed indestructible, 6'3" tall, football hero back home, a stern disciplinarian, physical fitness his specialty." Nicklin, who became the Battalion's Commanding Officer after the Normandy campaign, was killed in action during *Operation Varsity*. His replacement, Fraser Eadie, told reporters after the war that Nicklin "built up the Canadian Parachute Battalion.... When we reconciled our losses we found that we had lost the greatest guy that ever lived."

Canadian jumpmaster, Corporal Harris, briefs the Battalion Commanding Officer, Lieutenant-Colonel G.F.P. Bradbrooke, prior to the "Stand-Up."

Courtesy of the 1 Canadian Parachute Battalion Association Archives.

"Hardy tanned sons of Canada," observed Canadian reporters, were training in the United States. The arrangement "marked another expansion of the Canadian Army's training and another example of the cooperation between the two countries in the fight against the common enemy."

Courtesy of the 1 Canadian Parachute Battalion Association Archives.

The adrenalin rush. Parachute training officer, Lieutenant Ron Henry described the exiting drill as follows:

Jumpmaster: Get Ready! .... Stand up! ... Hook up!

Jumpmaster: Sound off equipment check!

Candidates: 12ok, 11ok, 10ok, 9ok, 8ok, 7ok, 6ok, 5ok, 4ok, 3ok, 2ok, 1ok,

Jumpmaster: Are you all Ok!

Candidates: Yes!

Jumpmaster: Then close up and stand at the door!

Candidates: Yes!

Jumpmaster: Away you go!

The parachute descent — the final test in earning the coveted "Jump Wings." A total of five jumps was required to earn the American Army Parachute Badge. Army journalist Sergeant Clyde Irvine wrote, "They are all very young and very fit and wildly delirious at the thought of having passed their gruelling tests."

Courtesy of the 1 Canadian Parachute Battalion Association Archives.

Courtesy of the 1 Canadian Parachute Battalion Association Archives.

Courtesy of the 1 Canadian Parachute Battalion Association Archives.

Courtesy of the Canadian Airborne Forces Museum.

In the spirit of the Fort Benning slogan, "We Ride to Fight — Why Walk?"

Courtesy of the Canadian Airborne Forces Museum.

Private Gord McKean provides an excellent portrait of Canada's early paratrooper training in Fort Benning. Note Canadian battledress, jump helmet, Sten gun and reserve chute.

Photographer Ken Bell, National Archives of Canada, Accession 1967-052, Z-1316-4.

On 8 March 1943 Lieutenant-Colonel Bradbrooke and
35 officers and ORs took part in a demonstration jump
for the visiting Canadian Brigadier-General A.E. Nash.
After landing, Bradbrooke executed the proper procedure for rolling-up a parachute.

All photos courtesy of the 1 Canadian Parachute Battalion Association Archives.

Graduation parade of 1 Canadian Parachute Battalion candidates who passed their basic parachutist course, held in Fort Benning, on 8 March 1943. Dignitaries in attendance included: Brigadier-General Walter S. Fulton, Commandant of Fort Benning, Brigadier G.P. Howell, Commandant of the Parachute School and Canadian Brigadier A.E. Nash. The candidates received their Canadian "Jump Wings." The Battalion's War Diary recorded that "comments about the way they swang [sic] their arms and kept the step could be heard.... Applause was ringing in everyone's ears throughout the whole affair uniting us still closer as a unit and as a team."

THE NEW INFANTRY MARCH

Airborne, we fly the sky
Paratroopers, we do or die
Speed troops, like the wind we go
We're sons o'guns! We're sons o'guns!
We won't take "no" for an answer,
Can't stop those paratroops,
Hurdling down into the fray.
Oh! It's not the way it used to be,
A bigger and better infantry comes in
    by air today!

It used to be the infantry did nothing,
    but march all day,
Dusty guys, with mud in their eyes,
Went slugging along the way.
But times have changed and now we range
The sky and sea of blue,
We ski a bit or maybe we'll hit the silk
    of a parachute. OH!!!

Courtesy of the 1 Canadian Parachute Battalion Association Archives.

Returning Home.

An aerial view of Camp Shilo, Manitoba. Various training apparatuses such as jumping and tumbling platforms and dummy fuselages can be seen. In addition, located on the outskirts of the wooded area are a series of climbing and agility stations. The total cost of building A-35, not including equipment and workshops, was approximately $380,000. The Battalion reported to its new training base in April 1943.

Major R.F. Routh, first Commanding Officer of the S-14 Canadian Parachute Training School, standing in front of the brand new 250-foot High Tower.

Photographer Ken Bell, National Archives of Canada, PA 201312.

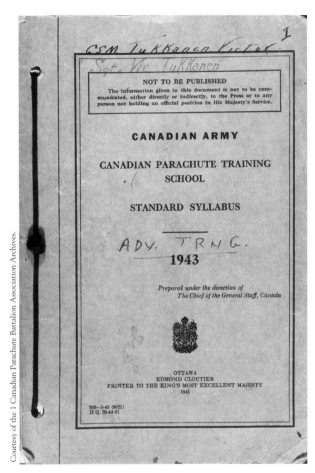

The Canadian Parachute Training School Standard Syllabus, 1943.

Due to its expanded training role, the S-14 Canadian Parachute Training School was redesigned as the A-35 Canadian Parachute Training Centre by NDHQ on 11 September 1943. The name change was officially implemented at Camp Shilo on 17 September. Nonetheless, it had a very questionable future. Canadian Military Headquarters in England consistently questioned the Centre's relevance. They felt greater efficiency could be realized by sending trainees directly to Fort Benning or Ringway instead of first qualifying them in Shilo, and then passing them on for conversion training in England.

Courtesy of the 1 Canadian Parachute Battalion Association Archives.

Courtesy of the 1 Canadian Parachute Battalion Association Archives.

Photographer Frank Royal, National Archives of Canada, PA 209725

Photographer unknown, National Archives of Canada, PA 209732.

The facilities for the paratroopers now reflected the standard and permanency of the more conventional Army units. 1 Canadian Parachute Battalion now had a visible presence in Canada. This series of photographs depicts the unit's barracks, quarters, and one of its messes in Shilo.

Photographer Frank Royal, National Archives of Canada, PA 209725

On 26 April 1942, a contingent of one hundred paratroopers participated in the Fourth Victory Loan Parade, in Winnipeg. This was the first real exposure of the Battalion to the public eye. Subsequently, they travelled to Toronto, Ottawa, and Montreal.

This contingent was also the first to receive the distinctive airborne headdress, the maroon beret, as well the Canadian Parachute Corps plastic cap badge. It was issued to individuals, such as Sergeant Stahl, prior to the parade in Winnipeg, 26 April 1943.

Photographer Lieutenant Strathy E. Smith, National Archives of Canada, PA 179772.

Courtesy of the 1 Canadian Parachute Battalion Association.

Canadian paratrooper at Camp Shilo. The pride is evident. "Here was a program," insisted Lieutenant-Colonel Fraser Eadie, "that developed some of the best soldiers I ever saw. Not to take anything away from other units but here we had a group that could put the Canadian Army on the map."

Courtesy of the 1 Canadian Parachute Battalion Association Archives.

On 4 May 1943, ten Battalion officers formed the first stick of paratroopers to jump in Canada. The three jumpmasters were Captain John Fauquier, Sergeant-Major A.T. Clifton, and Sergeant Darrel Harris. They were transported by truck to Rivers Air Base, Manitoba, located 45 miles away. Once they arrived, they adjusted their T5 parachute assemblies and emplaned in Lockheed Lodestar # 560. The weather conditions were ideal. Flight-Lieutenant C.H.P Killick R.C.A.F., a Canadian pilot who underwent special parachute-delivery flight training in Fort Benning, and co-pilot Flight-Lieutenant T.E. Daniels of Los Angeles, flew the plane. As the plane approached Drop Zone Proctor, it slowed down from 175 to 105 mph. At 0915 hours, the paratroopers exited the aircraft within a five second period at an altitude of 1,200 feet. All landed without mishap onto the DZ located approximately one mile south of Camp Shilo. The first paratrooper to land on Canadian soil was Lieutenant John (Steamer) Hanson.

Photographer Public Relations Office, M.D. 10, Winnipeg, National Archives of Canada, PA 209385.

The first "Wings Parade" was held on 13 September 1943 at the A-35 Canadian Parachute Training Centre. Lieutenant-General K. Stuart, the Chief of the General Staff (CGS), presided over this historic event pinning the "Jump Wings'" on 33 candidates, while Lieutenant-Colonel G.S. Currie, Deputy Minister of National Defence, handed out the jump certificates.

Photographer Public Relations Office, M.D. 10, Winnipeg, National Archives of Canada, PA 209386.

Photographer Public Relations Office, M.D. 10, Winnipeg, PPCLI Archives.

Following the "Wings Parade" Stuart addressed the new paratroopers and stated that he was extremely pleased in seeing that the candidates obviously enjoyed their training and that the instructors knew their jobs. The CGS then further elaborated on what was expected of airborne troops. "You'll be in the forefront of everything, but you'll never be left there for long.... Sometimes in strange country and in darkness you won't be landed in the right spot. In Sicily, many airborne troops were landed some distance from their objectives though enough were always landed to do the job. But those who were landed at a distance didn't sit down. Because they had such a grand fighting spirit, they went after the enemy who were nearest and created so much chaos behind the enemy lines that they materially assisted the work of the troops who came in later. That's what is expected of airborne troops."

A painful consistency. The unrelenting standard for physical fitness did not waiver from that imposed in Fort Benning. It was understood by all that "the single purpose behind an exceptionally tough training agenda is to weed out the timid, the weak and the unfit." Sergeant Irvine observed that "That eight weeks of tough advanced training weeds out those who can't or won't take it. It shows up the guy who wanted wings and a maroon beret and high brown boots — and no fighting.... It gets rid of the phonies before they jump, and not — as was formerly the case — afterwards."

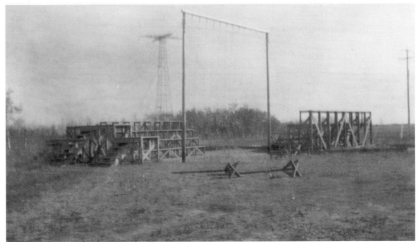

The location may have changed, but technique and equipment did not. Nonetheless, one major difference did exist — the less hospitable winter climate. Not surprisingly, this was not allowed to interfere with the requirement to train Canada's "sky warriors."

The first High Tower free flight in Canada. The first trial jumps from the High Tower were carried out by No. 1 Airborne Research and Development Centre (No. 1 ARDC) instructors in October 1945. The centre was an interim Airborne establishment created following the closing of A-35 CPTC and the setting up of the Joint Air School at Rivers, Manitoba. No. 1 ARDC staff tested new types of parachutes and airborne equipment and ran jumpmaster and parachute rigger courses.

Courtesy of the 1 Canadian Parachute Battalion Association Archives.

Although the parachute-training centre was running at capacity, the decision to send 1 Canadian Parachute Battalion overseas in the spring of 1943 placed additional stress on the Canadian airborne program. The Battalion was already under-strength and estimated wastage rates due to combat operations would only add to this deficiency. With this sense of urgency in mind, the training program pressed on.

Wind Machine training in Shilo, August 1944. This device was used to train and practise the aspiring paratroopers in the art of collapsing their parachutes on landing in high winds.

All photos courtesy of the 1 Canadian Parachute Battalion Association Archives.

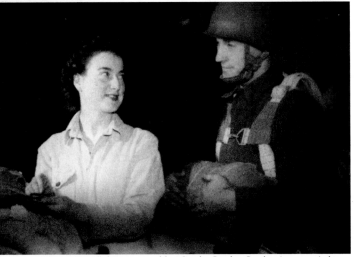

All photos courtesy of the 1 Canadian Parachute Battalion Association Archives.

One fundamental change in the Canadian parachute-training program was the deletion of parachute packing as a component of the Basic Parachutist Course. This function was eventually taken over and performed by eleven members of the Canadian Women's Army Corps (CWAC). They arrived at A-35 CPTC in small groups starting May 1943. Following an intensive course and examination, the new qualified packers (referred to by A-35 personnel as Para CWACs) took over this operation and worked out of the packing hangar facing the East Road. "The girls realize to the full the importance of their work" wrote a reporter of *The Heavenly Jerk*, the A-35 newspaper, "and spare no effort whatsoever to do it as well as they possibly can. And very frankly their packing is far superior to some of that seen in the old days, when qualified men would stuff the silk in the pack any old way." As time passed, the CWACs were given additional responsibilities. "Maintenance is very well equipped with the materials and facilities for making every possible kind of repair — and could, if required make complete chutes. CWACs were also employed at this work. After taking a packer's course they receive full and complete instructions on how to use and care for various types of sewing machines, and how to make any type of repair which may become necessary." Private Marjorie Parry was one of the first CWACs to qualify as a parachute packer.

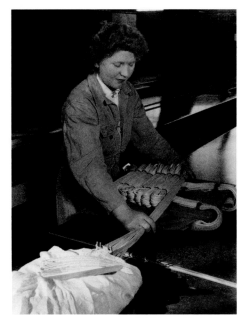

Lieutenant-General K. Stuart receives a technical briefing from Lieutenant A.L. Liddiard on the parachute's suspension lines during his 13 September 1943 visit to the A-35 CPTC.

Innovation and experimentation was an integral component of the Canadian airborne program.

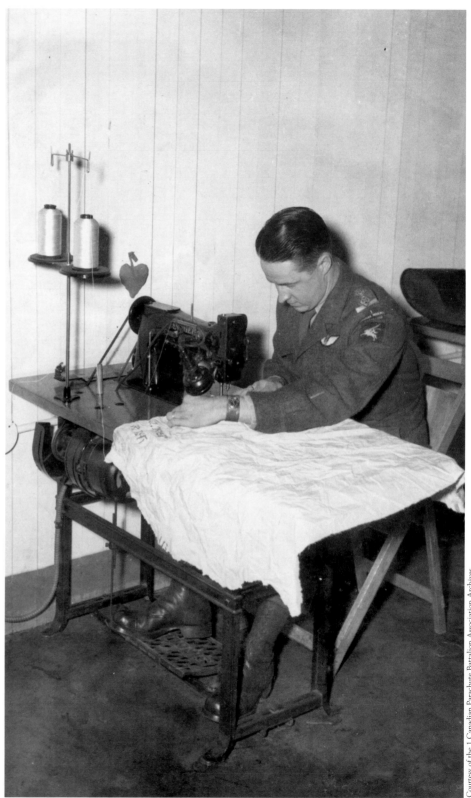

Courtesy of 1 Canadian Parachute Battalion Association Archives. Photographer Ken Bell, Negative Z-1889-23.

This mindset was most evident in the testing and experimentation of Allied weapons, uniforms, equipment, and doctrine.

Major D.H. Taylor replaced Lieutenant-Colonel R.F. Routh as Commanding Officer of A-35 CPTC on 26 May 1944. Taylor, a member of the Battalion in England, brought with him new rigorous airborne training techniques devised by Brigadier James Hill, Commander of 3 Parachute Brigade. Taylor immediately restructured the A-35 training syllabus. "It was taken for granted there [England] that any man could do the jumping," stated Taylor to a reporter of The Heavenly Jerk, "but not every one could stand up to the rigorous demands made by such a unit on its personnel in the field." As a result, all aspiring paratroopers now had to undertake an eight-week infantry course. Upon successful completion, the candidates were then authorized to take the three-week parachute course.

Of the many important lessons learned in England, the most important were to monitor the paratroopers closely and test them continuously. Taylor ensured this was done. One journalist reported, "And as the field training speeded up and tactical exercises became more the order of the day, the C.O. (Taylor) was to be seen at almost every one. Jumping with a stick, whizzing in his jeep from bombing attacks by aircraft which aimed at everything in sight, challenging sentries half-way through cold and rainy nights, the word quickly got round that whenever training was going on the C.O. was bound to be there."

TEN COMMANDMENTS OF THE CANADIAN PARACHUTE TROOPS

1. You are the elite of the Canadian Army. For you action shall be fulfilment and you must train yourself to stand every test.

2. Cultivate true comradeship, for together with your comrades you will triumph or die.

3. Be shy of speech and incorruptible. The strong act; the weak chatter, will bring you to the grave.

4. Calmness and caution, thoroughness and determination, valour and a relentless spirit of attack will make you superior when the test comes.

5. Face to face with the enemy, the most precious thing is ammunition. The man who fires aimlessly merely to reassure himself has no guts. He is a weakling and does not deserve the name of "Paratrooper."

6. Never Surrender. Your honour lies in victory or death.

7. Only with good weapons can you achieve success. Look after them therefore, on the principle, "First my weapons, then myself."

8. You must grasp the full meaning of each operation so that, even if your leader should fall, you can carry it out coolly and warily.

9. Fight chivalrously against an honourable foe; fifth columnist and civilian snipers deserve no quarter.

10. With your eyes open, keyed up to the highest pitch, agile as a greyhound, tough as leather, hard as steel, you will be the embodiment of a Canadian Paratrooper.

Source: Canadian Army Training Memorandum, No. 24, March 1943

A close-knit group of paratroopers in Camp Shilo, 1943.

(L to R) Major Adam Fauquier, Second-in-Command (2IC) A-35 CPTC and OC Parachute Training Wing and Lieutenant-Colonel Don Taylor, CO A-35 CPTC on the steps of the Officers Mess in Shilo, summer 1944.

The unit was soon recognized for its distinctiveness. Journalists reinforced the romantic as well as the hazardous nature of airborne warfare. One account stated, "Canada's most daring and rugged soldiers will assemble here soon, to be the envy of the thousands quartered on this vast plain — daring because they'll be training as paratroops: rugged because paratroops do the toughest jobs in hornet nests behind enemy lines."

New Canadian Training Direction for Airborne Troops.

Upon taking command of the A-35 CPTC, Major D.H. Taylor established a new training philosophy for paratroopers. He stated:

The public's conception of a parachutist is either that he is a slightly crazed individual or an exceedingly brave one. Jumping deliberately from an airplane is so foreign to normal behaviour that it seems natural to try to explain it by claiming the jumper abnormal. The exceedingly brave explanation often exists in the mind of some men who volunteer for this branch of service. A few weeks training and, they think, they too will qualify for a certificate of heroism. Such fine dreams are quickly banished from their minds when they report here. Publicity has placed the emphasis on the jump from the aircraft. Actually, the jump is about 2% of the training. The real accent should be placed on the ground training, on the physical fitness side. [What A-35 now stresses] is rigorous ground training that will turn out the toughest ground infantrymen in the world. Men who are good, tough soldiers first; jumpers second. The toughness required of a parachutist cannot be overestimated. Men can't quit road marches because they're tired. Overseas they march until there's blood in their boots, but they won't quit. They're required to cover 20 miles in 4 hours, 100 miles in 85 hours, swim 100 yards in full pack, carrying grenades, Bren Guns and ammo. So unless they show the stuff here they are returned to units, which do not require the same high standards of stamina and guts. Often it is impossible to drop parachutes on the exact spot at night. They may be 5 or 20 miles from their objective with too few minutes to get to it. Well, he's got to be there on time and ready to fight and can't do it if he's not in the best possible physical condition. It is conceivable too, that the nature of his work behind enemy lines will separate him from his own force for a couple of days and more. If he's going to get through and do a job he will have to be a top trained man with more than ordinary endurance. With this in mind, then a new training policy has been adopted here. Men go through an 8-week ground-training course without seeing a parachute.

Only after successfully completing it and being judged worthy of parachute training do they advance to a three-week course on 'chute. Like anything else that is new, parachute training had to go through its growing pains. For some time it had been the practise to send men into parachute training immediately upon their arrival here with ground training in the wake. That method turned out some glamour boys, the kind of guys who walk down the street flashing their parachute wings. No one should go away with this idea, however, that a parachutist shouldn't be proud of his jumps wings. He has every right to be proud of them, but just as much for a very tough ground training he undergoes as for challenging the angles with every jump.

Robert Noble from the Toronto Star witnessed some of the paratroopers on exercise and wrote an article that reflected his awe. "Part-airman, part-commando and part-engineer," he explained, "the purpose of the paratrooper is to be a land fighter after he leaps from the skies — an airborne soldier.... Barb wire entanglements, bridges, pillboxes and strongly erected dummy houses all fall, or are raised high in the air and completely demolished, as the advancing airborne soldiers inch in toward the objective."

Undeniably, the training focus was to create an aggressive, efficient, and fearless fighting machine. Sergeant Irvine, writing for *Khaki* magazine, believed that the airborne training was "designed to land a man behind the enemy lines — a man equipped to do more, and do it longer, than any other type of soldier." This was not an uncommon image. James Anderson from *Saturday Night* wrote "your Canadian paratrooper is an utterly fearless, level thinking, calculating killer possessive of all the qualities of a delayed-action time bomb." A later edition of the same periodical added that "a paratrooper's job is a tough one, for he floats down into unknown territory, but on the other hand, once he lands safely he usually has time to 'dig-in' before the enemy discovers him. For the enemy finds it impossible to establish any fixed defences against these air commandos."

All photos: Photographer unknown, National Archives of Canada, PA 209722-31, and PA 209697.

Parachute training was conducted at the A-35 CPTC throughout the entire course of the war regardless of season or climatic condition. Successful candidates were then sent to England as parachute reinforcements where they underwent further intensive airborne training with 1 Canadian Parachute Training Battalion.

Photographer unknown, National Archives of Canada, PA 197532.

Despite Major Taylor's new emphasis on ground training, the parachute component was still the major focal point for aspiring paratroopers.

All photos courtesy of the 1 Canadian Parachute Battalion Association Archives.

The Lockheed Lodestar was the primary transport aircraft used by A-35 CPTC. Its limited availability restricted the level of training conducted. It was fundamentally used only for basic parachute qualification training only. A major shortcoming of this aircraft was that it could take only eight jumpers at a time, instead of the 24 that a C-47 Dakota could carry. When A-35 opened, there was only one Lodestar (No. 560) available. It was a temperamental aircraft that constantly required mechanical work — so much so that the crew named the aircraft *The Gremlin Castle*. In August 1943, the aircraft spent more time in the repair hangar than in the air. To correct this frustrating situation, A-35 was allotted two additional Lodestars, on 10 December 1943. Their arrival helped accelerate the parachute qualifications phases and on occasion were used to drop paratroopers on airborne exercises. Later, in 1945, another two Lodestars increased the fleet to a total of five aircraft. They were based at Rivers Airport, No. 1 Central Navigation School and designated as No. 2 Detachment of No. 165 Squadron, Transport Command, R.C.A.F.

Courtesy of the 1 Canadian Parachute Battalion Association Archives.

Courtesy of the 1 Canadian Parachute Battalion Association Archives.

Sergeant Harris — jumpmaster at the A-35 CPTC.

Ed Brokofski, the jumpmaster observes the deployment of canopies from a "stick" of paratroopers that have exited the aircraft.

The Lodestar presented yet another problem. On take-off the eight jumpers (sometimes as many as sixteen) and two jumpmasters were required to stand up and push to the front of the aircraft to ensure that its centre of gravity was as far forward as possible. This enabled the pilot to get the tail off the ground. After reaching a respectable altitude, everyone would return to their seats on the benches.

An element of fear was always present, even though some could hide their trepidations better than others. James Anderson, a reporter for the *Winnipeg Tribune*, wrote, "I saw colour drain from the men's faces until they were almost white. I saw them get sick. It wasn't fear, just butterflies; just tension which built up and up."

The Drop Zone marker that indicated the forward edge of the DZ for pilots.

Canopies over the prairies. A familiar sight in the Camp Shilo vicinity. Between 11 September 1943 and 30 June 1945, 1,812 candidates divided into 63 classes took part in 13,335 live drops: 11,991 daylight and 1,344 night descents. The chronicler of A-35 CPTC nostalgically recorded the last qualifying drop: "Today, saw the winding up of the jump training, in the P.T.W. The final jump had been held up for a couple of days due to weather conditions, but today 108 men and Lieutenant R.E. Stewart qualified. They are probably the last men who will become parachutists in Canada at least during this war or unless the picture changes."

The same properties of the canopy that allowed for a safe descent often created problems for the jumper once on the ground.

The uniqueness and infancy of the new airborne method of warfare attracted a constant stream of visitors to the A-35 CPTC.

Parachute maintenance — the drying of canopies after a drop.

PART III

THE BRITISH EXPERIENCE

On 20 July 1943, 30 Battalion officers and 543 other ranks boarded the 84,000 ton British liner the *Queen Elizabeth,* en route to the UK. This was the world's largest ship and passenger vessel and could transport up to 14,867 personnel per voyage. "Our company," recalled Boyd Anderson, "went down the stairway to what was called the 'D' Deck, deep in the bowels of the ship, right at the water level next to the powerful diesel motors that powered this gigantic ship. For the remainder of that day and two more days, more and more military personnel arrived and a steady stream of men and women came down the gangplank and disappeared somewhere into this huge carrier. We were told that this one ship and crew of one thousand would carry twenty thousand or more persons overseas. On board one ship we had a population almost as great as that of Moose Jaw. The crew told us that we had no escort. Because of the ship's speed and because we would change directions continuously the submarines would not be a threat.... On the fifth day we passed Ireland and the water was green, the way I had read or been told it would be. We now had air cover and there was no more zig-zagging by the *Queen Elizabeth.* She opened up her motors and headed straight for Greenock, Scotland.... [which] was on an estuary next to the ocean. We did not dock, but were taken off the ship to land in smaller boats. It is my understanding that the *Queen Elizabeth* kept her power up [so that] if necessary, [she could] head out for the high sea and safety in a matter of minutes."

Photographer Lieutenant C.E. Nye, National Archives of Canada, PA 205353.

Photographer Lieutenant C.E. Nye, National Archives of Canada, PA 209733.

Photographer Laurie A. Audrain, National Archives of Canada, PA 205354.

The Minister of Defence, J.L. Ralston, inspects the newly arrived Canadian paratroopers at No. 1 Canadian Base Staging Camp, in Chobham, Surrey, 3 August 1943.

Photographer Captain Malindine, Imperial War Museum. H38770.

Lieutenant-General F.A.M. Browning, C.B. D.S.O., had been a driving force behind the development of British Parachute and Air Landing units since the summer of 1940 when the Prime Minister called for the establishment of a corps of paratroops numbering 5,000. Browning's demanding standards and training techniques paid off great dividends during the course of British airborne operations conducted in North Africa from December 1942 to April 1943. The Germans were so impressed by the stamina, resiliency, and determination displayed by Browning's paratroopers that they referred to them as *Rote Teufel* — "Red Devils." Later Browning stated, "Such distinctions are seldom given in war, and then only to the finest troops." Many of these now battle-tested British paratroopers would later provide valuable instruction on airborne warfare to the members of 1 Canadian Parachute Battalion.

While inspecting his Canadian unit, Brigadier Hill observed that he had before him a diamond in the rough. "I soon felt," Hill later wrote, "that I was on the same wave-length as the Battalion, for they were similar in so many ways to the original British 1st Parachute Battalion which I had commanded."

Photographer Sergeant E.R. Bonter, National Archives of Canada, PA 209694.

Photographer Sergeant E.R. Bonter, National Archives of Canada, PA 209695.

Photographer unknown, National Archives of Canada, PA 209692.

The metamorphosis begins. Canadian paratroopers adopt a distinctive airborne appearance. On 10 August 1943, Canadian paratroopers were ordered to dye all their "Battle Order" equipment in a dark green colour. In addition, 20–21 August, they were issued British Airborne items of dress. These included the camouflage pattern Denison smock, the parachute over-smock, the airborne steel helmet and helmet netting, the string vest, and a second pair of black ankle boots. All the outerwear had been specifically designed to insure the paratroopers' personal safety during the jumping and parachute deployment phases. Furthermore, the smock's camouflage pattern, colour scheme, and helmet cover textures enabled the paratroopers to blend in with the vegetation and terrain and "disappear" seconds after vacating the Drop Zone. Also, extra pockets and special webbing increased the paratrooper's ability to carry a larger combat load. Additional quantities of ammunition and supplies enabled operational self-reliance, independence, and flexibility over an undetermined period of time. It was never lost on the paratroopers that once on the ground, they were on their own until ground forces linked up. With the new order of dress, it was only the distinctive Canadian Parachute Badge sewn over the left breast pocket of the Denison smock that identified the wearer as being a Canadian, and therefore, a member of 1 Canadian Parachute Battalion. They also wore the golden shoulder slip-on identification strip that identified them as members of the 6 Airborne Division.

The Canadian paratroopers arrived at their new home in Bulford Camp on 11 August 1943. "Our Battalion," commented Boyd Anderson, a "B" Company veteran, "was billeted in Carter Barracks located on Salisbury Plains. We were about fifteen miles from Salisbury, well known for its famous Cathedral built in the thirteenth century. Another historical structure a few miles from us was the famous Stonehenge." About the accommodations, Anderson said, "The rooms were very comfortable with bathroom facilities inside the barracks. Every platoon of thirty men had a barrack room to itself and at the entrance from the hallway there was a room for the two senior corporals. The junior corporals' bunks were in the barracks room with the privates. The sergeants had their own quarters as did the officers."

The first two weeks of August were spent re-organiz-
ing the Battalion and completing a series of administrative procedures. Brigadier Hill officially welcomed
the Canadians to 3 Parachute Brigade and gave a brief
outline of what he expected of them. Training commenced shortly thereafter. Boyd Anderson recalled
that from the very outset, a very competitive atmosphere was instilled in every phase of training. "There
was a fierce competition to be the best Battalion in
the brigade," he recalled, "and then the best company, the best platoon and finally the best section. Good
military organization and good morale and discipline
were built on competition."

Royal Air Force Station Ringway. In the aftermath of British Prime Minister Winston Churchill's June 1940 directive to raise a corps of 5,000 parachute troops, it was decided to create an Airborne Forces training centre in Ringway Airport, Manchester. This establishment was originally named Central Landing School. However, in August 1940, it was renamed Central Landing Establishment and later yet changed again to No. 1 Parachute Training School, Royal Air Force Station Ringway. Contrary to the American parachute training that was conducted in one facility, the British divided their parachute training into two distinctive phases given in two separate locations. The initial selection and preparatory physical ground work was carried out at the Airborne Forces Depot, Hardwick Hall near Chesterfield in Derbyshire. Successful candidates were then sent for parachute training and a series of qualifying jumps from a static balloon (2 descents) and finally from a converted Armstrong-Whitworth Whitley bomber (5 descents).

Photographer Sergeant E.R. Bonter, National Archives of Canada, PA 211198, PA 209698, and PA 209699.

Between 9 September 1943 and 25 September 1944, 1,160 Canadian paratroopers underwent British parachute conversion training at PTS Ringway. Private Jan de Vries was part of the first group and his eight qualifying jumps (static balloon and aircraft) were logged in his Soldier's Book.

In September 1943, all 1 Canadian Parachute Battalion personnel was sent in groups to Ringway to undergo the British parachute conversion course. Preliminary training was conducted to instil the correct exiting procedures from a tight three-foot opening. "The proper way to jump," explained Trooper Wilfred Gregory, a member of the original Ringway group, "is stiffly as though you are standing at attention. Paratroopers leave quickly that way — less than a second apart." This training phase was then followed up by two parachute qualification jumps from a static balloon and five qualification jumps from a converted Whitley bomber.

In Britain, candidates conducted their first jumps by exiting through a hole in the floor of a gondola attached to a static balloon. (This was vastly different from training in the United States, where all jumps were made from aircraft, specifically the C-47 Dakota, using a side-door exit.) Having mastered these individual exits, paratroopers then moved on to in-flight jumping from a converted Whitley bomber.

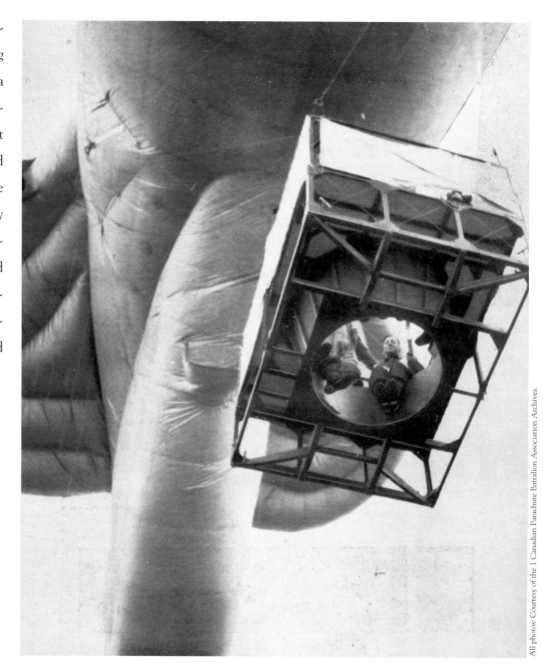

The psychological and technical approach to parachute training in Britain differed from that in the U.S. "In their instruction to prospective paratroopers," writes Boyd Anderson, "the British played down the manly part of jumping. They told us that many Russian women were jumpers and assured us that many British nurses had already qualified. They said that jumping in itself was easy and that our troubles would start after we were committed to action. They seemed to believe that good training, strict discipline, leadership, and intelligence were important along with good physical conditioning." The technical approach to British parachuting also varied. The Canadians now jumped with only a main parachute and no reserve. They exited through a hole in the floor of the fuse-lage and were taught a different landing drill. In the U.S., the Canadians were taught to land with their feet shoulder-width apart. The British, on the other hand, landed feet and knees together, with legs slightly bent. Upon landing, the U.S.-trained paratrooper was instructed to execute a forward roll, ending up in a foetal position. The British method allowed for the body to better absorb the impact of landing. This also greatly reduced the amount of ankle and leg injuries. The Americans eventually adopted the British approach. Another dramatic difference noted by the Canadians was the philosophy of instruction. The British parachute instructors (PIs) encouraged individuals, and aimed to pass as many as possible. Conversely, the Americans PIs "discouraged" the volunteers and tried to get as many to quit as possible, stressing that only the toughest could become paratroopers.

Photographer Sergeant E.R. Bonter, National Archives of Canada, PA 191121.

Photographer Sergeant E.R. Bonter, National Archives of Canada, PA 204959.

Lieutenant Richard Hilborn has his harness release checked by British Lieutenant, the Honourable Hugh Fraser (brother of famous commando Lord Lovat). The Battalion utilized the British "X"-Type Parachute for all their parachute conversion and refresher training, as well as their later exercise jumps. The parachute was activated by a static line and once deployed provided the paratrooper with a 28-foot diameter canopy. Twenty-eight rigging lines were attached to four main straps that were secured to the harness. On top on the canopy was a 22-inch vent, which assisted in the stabilization of the oscillation.

Private George Wright, a member of the first Ringway group, had the opportunity of training in both the UK and the US parachute systems. He preferred the British parachute harness. "The British parachutes," he argued, "had a quick trip button located in our belly button area. You gave it a hard slap and half turn just before landing and your chute harness falls off. In the States they had a snap on system and you couldn't shed your harness easily."

Courtesy of the 1 Canadian Parachute Battalion Association Archives.

1 Canadian Parachute Battalion officers wearing British "X"-Type parachutes. In Britain, the paratroopers were not outfitted with a reserve parachute. There were three reasons for this. Firstly, the British dropped their paratroopers from a lower altitude — 800 feet comparatively to 1,000 to 1,500 feet in the United States. This low altitude did not give the paratrooper enough time to activate his reserve. Secondly, there was a three-foot "exit" hole in the floor of the various British aircraft. Quite simply, a paratrooper with a reserve and his other equipment, including his main parachute harness would never clear the opening. Finally, economics also came into play. Senior military commanders were reluctant to order the manufacture of reserve parachutes due to their high £60 per item cost.

The airborne soldier. Lieutenant-Colonel Fraser Eadie noted that "The soul of the unit which was reflected in the attitude and performance of the individual paratroopers always remained: to go a little farther; to move across country a little faster; to be a little more cunning."

"Our first jump was from a barrage balloon," explained Private George Wright, "to which was attached a basket hooked up to a three to four hundred foot line. Two candidates and one instructor would get in. In the centre or the floor was a three foot hole. On this first day the entire group jumped except one officer. After two jumps we graduated to the Whitley bomber. I felt safer in the balloon. You're stationary. Everything is safe and quiet. You are only two. It didn't seem frightening. A draft, a snap meant your chute opened and you floated gently to the ground. There was no big thrill in it. This was all explained to you during the training."

Later, in September 1943, when the Battalion underwent its conversion training, the balloon was elevated to 800 feet. The gondola carried six individuals, normally a combination of one to two instructors and four to five trainees. These qualification jumps were conducted either very early in the morning or after supper when the wind was normally at its lowest.

Courtesy of the 1 Canadian Parachute Battalion Association Archives.

Photographer Sergeant E.R. Bonter, National Archives of Canada, PA 204958.

Courtesy of the 1 Canadian Parachute Battalion Association Archives.

"A sloppy jump," explained Trooper Wilfred Gregory, "with arms waving or legs apart, is called a 'spider exit,' and a sloppy landing is called a 'ropy.' A 'pansy landing' is when you come down easy. If a fellow's parachute doesn't open, we say he's had a 'Roman Candle' or just that he's had it. That rarely happens."

Initially, Ringway evaluated two aircraft — the Armstrong-Whitworth "Whitley" Bomber and the Bombay Transport. The Whitley was chosen after a series of tests and an assessment of the aircraft's actual availability. The British conducted their first parachute jumps from the rear of the plane where the machine-gun turret had been removed. The results were disastrous. They then proceeded to remove the central floor machine-gun turret, which provided a tight three-foot opening. Private George Wright still vividly remembers his first Whitley jump. "We would go in with a ten man stick," he explained. "Half the stick would crawl into the front end of the plane, sit with their backs against the wall and feet in the centre of the plane. The other half would go towards the tail end of the aircraft. Static lines would be attached and would slide with you as you moved towards the hole. There were three coloured lights: red light would be on [during flight indicating no exit]; yellow would mean to get ready and on the green light you jumped. With the Whitley, you could not stand up due to the small fuselage, you were always in the sitting position.

"The drill would be that the man closest to the hole, from the front group, would swing his feet in the hole, sit on the edge and push off equally with both hands. Then the first man from the rear group would do the same. Each man from each group would shuffle and slide towards the hole and drop out. I would always like to be part of the stick, which would sit in the front of the plane. When you dropped out, you had your back to the slip stream, so you didn't get hit in the face. You would get hit in the back. The idea was to get your feet in the hole, shove off equally with your hands behind you, and drop straight out. It was very important to shove off equally, if not you would spin out of the hole, causing you to go into a spinning motion and this would cause your parachute to

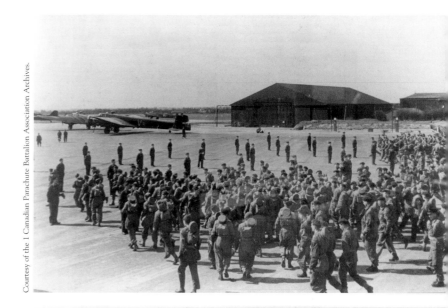

Courtesy of the 1 Canadian Parachute Battalion Association Archives.

Courtesy of the 1 Canadian Parachute Battalion Association Archives.

Photographer unknown, National Archives of Canada, PA 209691.

wind up and this would be called a Roman Candle. You had to avoid that. If you pushed off too hard, then you would crash into the other side of the hole and get a bloody nose."

Regardless whether it was a balloon or a aircraft exit, each man experienced his personal pre-jump jitters. Sergeant-Major W.J. "Knobby" Clark, a member of the original Ringway group and later the regimental sergeant-major of 1 Canadian Parachute Battalion, recalled the stress of his initial Whitley jump, which manifested itself in beads of perspiration forming on his right thumb. "I just sat there and looked at the stuff — couldn't do anything about it. Then I jumped. There is that moment of breathlessness when you wonder if your parachute will open. Then it does and you're on top of the world, just the way all the boys are.... Every jump is the thrill of a life-time. Nothing compares with it."

Another converted bomber used by the British parachute forces for airborne exercises and operations was the Armstrong-Whitmore Albemarle. The floor-exiting drill was similar to that used when jumping from a Whitley. For their drop as part of the invasion advance party in the early minutes of 6 June 1944, "C" Company, 1 Canadian Parachute Battalion used the Albemarle aircraft. The rest of the Battalion jumped from C-47 Dakota aircraft.

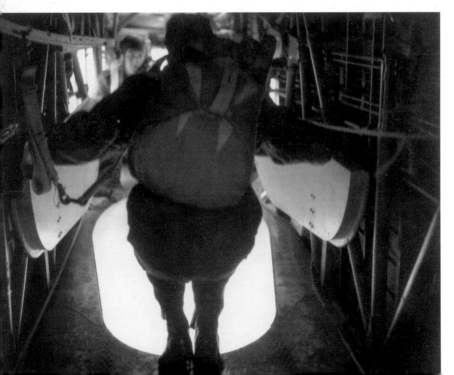

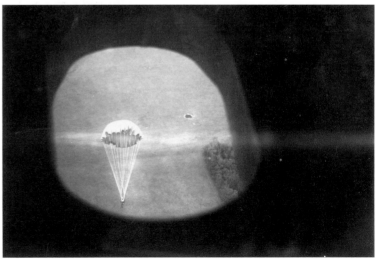

Photographers unknown, IWM, Negatives CH 12049, CH 13189, CH 13190, CH 13191.

Not surprisingly, the Canadian paratroopers' initial outlook and attitude to the conversion training sometimes lacked professionalism. According to Boyd Anderson, "About four hundred Fort Benning boys, "qualified to go to Ringway for the conversion course on British jumping methods. This is when we received our first set back. We were cocky, we had our American wings and brown boots, and we also had our Canadian wings. Most of our guys didn't take the British instruction seriously. Many of us were going to the nearby British pubs or into Manchester every night. We were out for good time. On the two first jumps some of our guys came down with their legs apart. The British instructors were very upset after our second jump. We were told very firmly that we must shape up or we would be shipped out. They would disqualify us....

Photographer unknown, National Archives of Canada, PA 209693.

After a shaky start we redeemed ourselves with our British instructors." Upon the course completion, Wing Commander Maurice Newman, D.F.C. presented Sergeant D.R. Reynolds, a member of the Canadian Film and Photo Unit, attached to the 1 Canadian Parachute Battalion, with "Jump Wings." These were to be distributed to graduating Canadian paratroopers who had successfully completed a total of five jumps from the Static Balloon and the Whitley Bomber.

Lieutenant Richard Hilborn exiting a Douglas C-47 Dakota during a training jump in England.

Photographer Sergeant E.R. Bonter, National Archives of Canada, PA 115865.

British paratrooper displaying standard infantry equipment (fall 1943) that was adopted by 1 Canadian Parachute Battalion in England. Distinctive to the paratroopers were the para helmet, Denison smock, and toggle rope. This paratrooper also carries a two-inch mortar.

Courtesy of the 1 Canadian Parachute Battalion Association Archives.

Photographer unknown, National Archives of Canada, PA 209696.

Photographer Sergeant E.R. Bonter, National Archives of Canada, PA 204957.

Courtesy of the 1 Canadian Parachute Battalion Association Archives.

During the months of August to November 1943 and again in 1944, great emphasis was placed on weapon qualifications. Because the airborne battleground was often behind enemy lines and fraught with resupply difficulties, Brigadier Hill insisted that each paratrooper be proficient in the use of small arms so that every round would count. Hill said that he would remind his Canadian paratroopers about the need for conservation whenever he visited the various ranges: "Due to a lack of ammunition, we always stressed the necessity of holding one's fire until the whites of the eyes could be seen." Numerous days were spent on different firing ranges.

In the 17 October 1943 entry in the Battalion's training syllabus, Lieutenant-Colonel G.F.P. Bradbrooke emphasized Hill's directives: "Ranges have been allotted for the complete week and it is expected that all personnel will do well. This can only be accomplished by spending all accounted time on the individual and weapons training. No man will be allowed to loiter or have his time unoccupied. Company Commanders will exercise strict supervision. A Staff Sergeant from Bisley will be attached to the unit commencing 10 October. He will be used exclusively for pointing out errors and making suggestions to improve the weapons training, and for all ranks 'to pick his brains,' to the ultimate in order that we may derive the greatest possible benefit from a well qualified N.C.O. who no doubt knows his job."

Within a few months the paratroopers had honed their marksmanship skills on an impressive selection of weapons: Lee-Enfield #4 Mark 1 with sniper scope; Lee-Enfield #4 Mark 1; Sten gun Mark 2 with silencer; Sten gun Mark 5 (Airborne Model); Browning PA M 1911 pistol; Browning 9mm; Enfield # 2 Mark 1 .380-calibre pistol; Bren Mark 1; PIAT (Projector infantry, anti-tank); two-inch mortar. Later in December, the Canadian paratroopers were introduced and familiarized on handling a variety of German weapons such as anti-tank rifles, machine guns, Schmeisser machine pistols, 50 mm and 81mm mortars and the M98 rifles.

Canadian paratroopers demonstrate handling drills for the Vickers machine gun and the three-inch mortar to a Chinese military mission at Bulford Camp.

Photographer Sergeant Laing, IWM, Negatives H 35521, H 35522.

The effect of the training very quickly became evident. Fraser Eadie, one of the company commanders at the time, reflected on the evolution. He observed, "the unit had pride that you could cut with a knife. The individuals had excellent infantry skills and an outstanding attitude. They were physically fit and extremely adaptable."

Sergeant Clyde Irvine, a writer for *Khaki* magazine, was one of many who were impressed with the varied and demanding training undertaken by the paratroopers. This tough regimen, he explained, was necessary because airborne forces were "designed to land a man behind the enemy lines — a man equipped to do more, and do it longer, than any other type of soldier."

Courtesy of the 1 Canadian Parachute Battalion Association Archives.

"Sweat saves Blood." Training in full gear in England shortly before D-Day. Left to right are Carl Banta, Phee, Nelson Macdonald, and Carl Baxter.

Courtesy of the 1 Canadian Parachute Battalion Association Archives.

First priority of the light infanteer — take care of your feet. Members of 1 Canadian Parachute Battalion take a rest during one of the many forced marches in England. From left to right are Haviland, Villeneuve, Shank.

Courtesy of the 1 Canadian Parachute Battalion Association Archives.

Courtesy of the 1 Canadian Parachute Battalion Association Archives.

Members of 1 Canadian Parachute Battalion pose for a picture following a training exercise in England at Carter Barracks. The paratroopers are wearing experimental load-carrying vests for Bren gun magazines.

Photographer unknown, National Archives of Canada, PA 206061.

The unconquerable airborne spirit is clearly reflected in this portrait of Andy J.J. McNally. Private Jan de Vries later recalled that "we had a feeling that whatever was required, we could do."

The bond forged through shared hardship and experience led Private T.A. Gavinski to believe, like many in the Battalion, that "it was a brotherhood ... the most wonderful thing that ever happened to me."

Her Majesty, Queen Elizabeth, speaks to Major D.J. Wilkins during an inspection of 1 Canadian Parachute Battalion on 19 May 1944.

Photographer Sergeant E.R. Bonter, National Archives of Canada, PA 193086.

Courtesy of the 1 Canadian Parachute Battalion Association Archives.

Photographer Sergeant E.R. Bonter, National Archives of Canada, PA 204960.

The Queen converses with British Sergeant Lower. Brigadier James Hill is in the background. Hill would later write, "I shall for ever remember with great pride, that I had the honour to have under my command, both in and out of battle, a Canadian Battalion which is regarded by all of us as, as fine a fighting unit as has ever left these shores."

Lieutenant-Colonel G.F.P. Bradbrooke, the CO of 1 Canadian Parachute Battalion, and the Queen observe a parachute deployment conducted by the members of 1 Canadian Parachute Training Battalion. These paratroopers would later be transferred to 1 Canadian Parachute Battalion to replace casualties incurred during operations. During this visit, the members of 1 Canadian Parachute Battalion were inspected by the King and Queen, and took part in various demonstrations that highlighted unit capability and equipment. The Battalion did not participate in the parachute drop in order to avoid possible injuries as the date for the D-Day operation approached.

Photographer Sergeant Morris, IWM, Negative H 38620.

Photographer Sergeant Morris, IWM, Negative H 38620.

Photographer unknown, National Archives of Canada, PA 179150.

Sniper demonstration for the Royal visit.

Courtesy of the 1 Canadian Parachute Battalion Association Archives.

Training run without equipment led by Lieutenant G.H. MacDonald, Bulford, England. Canadian paratroopers quickly adapted to the gruelling airborne training regimen enforced by Brigadier Hill.

Photographer Sergeant E.R. Bonter, National Archives of Canada, PA 179678.

Brigadier James Hill talks to (left to right) Captain R.A. MacDonald, Major P.R. Griffin (British airborne officers), and Major J.A. Nicklin, Bulford, England, 4 December 1943. Dan Hartigan recalled, "My first impression of Brigadier Hill was, here's a guy who meant business."

The Brigade Commander unquestionably earned the devotion of his Canadian charges. Private A.H. Carignan explained that "Brigadier Hill to this day, is the most inspirational military commander I've ever served under (including Korea and regular force army post war). His nerves of steel — moving around under intense fire to rally weak points under attack — are legendary and the care and consideration for those under him inspired undying loyalty and affections."

Members of 6 Airborne Division participated in numerous experimental trial jumps to test a new piece of equipment known as the Leg Kit Bag. Initially, the British dropped their support weapons, ammunition, and additional equipment in containers. However, it was quickly noted that such a delivery system separated the paratroopers from their much-needed equipment and weaponry. German operations at the beginning of the war also highlighted this critical flaw. Experiments were then conducted to devise a method of dropping the paratroopers with their equipment. Thus, Leg Kit Bags were devised and tested. Once the bag was loaded and closed, it was attached to the paratrooper's right leg with the bottom resting on the top of the foot. Prior to landing, a release mechanism was activated, freeing the kit bag from the jumper's leg. A twenty-foot rope then unravelled. This release drill was a tricky procedure because not only did the paratrooper have to prepare to land, he now also had to control the swinging motion caused by the heavy suspended kit bag. The discomfort of the extra weight and difficult flight following the bag's release was more than compensated for since the paratrooper now had immediate access to his equipment, heavy weaponry, and extra ammunition.

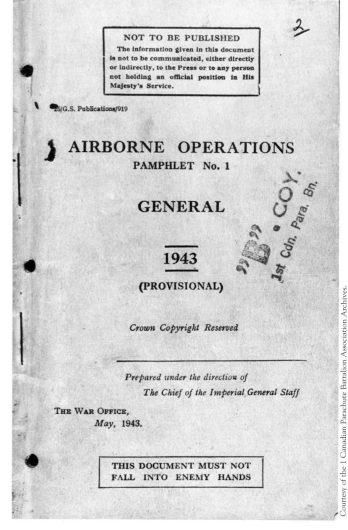

Courtesy of the 1 Canadian Parachute Battalion Association Archives.

Courtesy of the 1 Canadian Parachute Battalion Association Archives.

Courtesy of the 1 Canadian Parachute Battalion Association Archives.

Courtesy of the 1 Canadian Parachute Battalion Association Archives.

Loading a C-47 aircraft for a training jump in England. Army journalist Sergeant Irvine asserted that "by the time he [the paratrooper] lands on the enemy, he will be the toughest guy the Jerries have ever met — and, by the same token, he will be the finest type of all-round fighting man we can produce — a front line fighter with his feet firmly planted on the earth and his heart in the sky."

Courtesy of the 1 Canadian Parachute Battalion Association Archives.

The third dimension of war. James Anderson, a reporter for *Saturday Night* magazine, wrote, "So your paratroopers carry the front line with them. They slap it down behind enemy lines, outflank flanks, nip pincer moves. They're a new kind of fighting unit to put smashing blows in the enemy's rear by whatever method best presents itself: Sabotage, rumor, filtration tactics, or straight hammer-head blows."

Courtesy of the 1 Canadian Parachute Battalion Association Archives.

Mass drop during *Exercise Cooperation* in England, 7 February 1944. In preparation for D-Day, one of the aims of this exercise was to drop the maximum number of paratroopers in the smallest possible area in the shortest amount of time.

Courtesy of the 1 Canadian Parachute Battalion Association Archives.

Photographer unknown, National Archives of Canada, PA 206059

Photographer unknown, National Archives of Canada, PA 205058.

Courtesy of the 1 Canadian Parachute Battalion Association Archives.

The Battalion on exercise in England, winter 1943–1944. In regard to the paratrooper, journalist Clyde Irvine noted, "Any tiredness, any temptation to dog it will not be tolerated. His mind is conditioned and his body responds to swift, immediate action. A paratrooper must want to go overseas. He must have the heart that will sustain him when he is dropped in enemy territory alone or with his section, and when the odds are all against him."

Courtesy of the 1 Canadian Parachute Battalion Association Archives.

Courtesy of the 1 Canadian Parachute Battalion Association Archives.

After the jump and exercise in January 1944, members of 5 Platoon, "B" Company pose for a picture. (Front row) Sergeant John Kemp, D.S. Ticknor, W. Pauk, J.J. Melenius; (back row) V.H. Symons, D.A. Currie, E. Makela, W.A. Crowe.

Courtesy of the 1 Canadian Parachute Battalion Association Archives.

The ever-present "Meat" or "Blood Wagon," in the parlance of the paratroopers, was always a graphic reminder that, contrary to what many seemed to believe, they were not in fact immortal.

Photographer Sergeant E.R. Bonter, National Archives of Canada, PA 211199.

Airborne Forward Observation Officer (FOO) party exercising in England, spring 1944.

Courtesy of the 1 Canadian Parachute Battalion Association Archives.

Photographer Frank L. Duberville, National Archives of Canada, PA 137025.

Sergeant E.R. Bonter was one of the five photographers who underwent parachute training to document, for posterity, the various training phases, exercises, and operations conducted by 1 Canadian Parachute Battalion.

Courtesy of the 1 Canadian Parachute Battalion Association Archives.

On 24 May 1944, all personnel of 1 Canadian Parachute Battalion packed their belongings into kit bags and left them in front of their beds inside their respective barracks. The paratroopers took only webbing, ammunition, and weapons. Personnel then waited impatiently in front of their designated trucks.

"While the battalion was inspected," reminisces Dan Hartigan, "a few thoughtful soldiers who remained behind as supply troops had quietly tossed extra blankets aboard every transport truck, to be spread out on the floor to make the dice roll smooth.... Cigarettes came out and were dragged deeply as we anticipated the arrival of our Sergeant-Majors to move us out." And so, heavily laden airborne soldiers then embarked on the fifty-mile trip to their transit camp near the village of Down Ampney, located on a road between Cirencester and Poulton in Gloucester.

Hartigan remembers the chilling welcome given by a British regimental sergeant-major on arrival. He drew the attention of the Canadian paratroopers to a single strand of barbwire, strung out one metre off the ground in a field some distance from the tents. "You are now in a place called a security transit camp," he bellowed. "Here you are going to learn the best kept secrets in the world. Anyone who places a foot beyond the single strand of barbed wire will be shot without being challenged. Your best bet is not to go within a hundred feet of it."

Pictured are, left to right, RSM "Knobby" Clark, CSM Norbert Joseph and CSM Rollie Outhwaite.

PART IV

THE BATTALION AT WAR

Lieutenant-Colonel Bradbrooke speaks with Major P. Griffin and Lieutenant P. Rousseau prior to deploying to the airhead on 5 June 1944. Rousseau was killed in action the next day.

Courtesy of the 1 Canadian Parachute Battalion Association Archives.

1 Canadian Parachute Battalion officers deploying to the airhead on 5 June 1944.

Courtesy of the 1 Canadian Parachute Battalion Association Archives.

Final thoughts before departure. "B" Company platoon commanders, lieutenants P. Rousseau, N. Toseland, and Harrison, 5 June 1944.

Courtesy of the 1 Canadian Parachute Battalion Association Archives.

Courtesy of the 1 Canadian Parachute Battalion Association Archives.

Preparing to return to the continent. Pictured is a paratrooper from 1 Canadian Parachute Battalion, a unit that Prime Minister Winston Churchill referred to as "those formidable Canadians."

The calm before the storm — the D-Day transit camp. Private Alexandre Huton remembered, during an interview with L.S.B. Shapiro of *Maclean's* magazine, "it was pretty nerve-racking waiting for the signal that the party was really on. We were confident all right, but you know how it is when you've trained for and thought about a certain day for two years. You sort of get impatient when you know it's pretty close, and you can't wait for it to happen so it will be behind you and finished with. Well, we sat around those three days and smoked and played cards, but mostly we cleaned weapons over and over again and thought about the party."

Photographer Sergeant E.R. Bonter, National Archives of Canada, PA 209704-707.

Photographer Sergeant E.R. Bonter, National Archives of Canada, PA 209704-707.

Canadian paratroopers in their staging area prior to D-Day. Private N.V. Wilson and Sergeant B.D. Pym, from the "Victory Rifle Platoon," stand in the background with their distinctive haircuts. They were two of nine paratroopers who had their hair cut to spell out the word "Victory" in Morse code. Wilson and Pym sport the letters "V" and the "I" respectively.

Ready to pierce the Reich — 5 June 1944. One Canadian reporter wrote, "the sky soldiers were trained to a razor's edge when they piled into Royal Air Force Albermales and Douglas C-47 transport the night of 5 June."

Courtesy of the 1 Canadian Parachute Battalion Association Archives.

Courtesy of the 1 Canadian Parachute Battalion Association Archives.

This photograph was also taken 5 June prior to the invasion. Of the 19 paratroopers allocated to this aircraft, five would be killed, eight wounded, and two captured by the enemy.

The glider fields of Normandy.

An unidentified paratrooper on sentry at the outskirts of a wooded area, 6 June 1944. "I am proud," stated Private Mervin Jones, "and very glad I was part of the 1st Canadian Parachute Battalion Airborne Invasion of France. But I would never, never do it again ... jumping out of an airplane into black space towards a land full of the enemy.... There are no front lines at a time like this; there were Germans all over the place ... you could be among any number of them."

Photographer Sergeant D.A. Reynolds, National Archives of Canada, PA 209703.

Courtesy of the 1 Canadian Parachute Battalion Association Archives.

The Robehomme Bridge, Normandy, France. This was the D-Day objective of 5 Platoon, "B" Company.

A brief rest following the battle at Varaville in Normandy, 6 June 1944. Army journalist Sergeant Irvine wrote, "Plummeting from the skies near Caen last June the 1st Canadian Parachute Battalion fell on the German garrison like a plague of armoured devils. Hundreds of them — hundreds of the finest infantry men Canada has ever produced."

Courtesy of the 1 Canadian Parachute Battalion Association Archives.

Courtesy of the 1 Canadian Parachute Battalion Association Archives.

Composite/panoramic photograph taken from Lance-Corporal John Ross's trench in front of the gatehouse at Varaville. The picture shows Germans surrendering on the left side of the picture, and being disarmed on the right side.

Canadian paratroopers dig in along a road in Normandy, France, 8 June 1944. Sir Huw Weldon, author of *Red Berets in Normandy,* wrote, "One of the most intense areas of concentration was near Brigade Headquarters where the 1st Canadian Parachute Battalion was involved in a series of deadly encounters. Although the battalion was entirely Canadian, they were very much part of the British 6th Airborne Division. The Battalion, 600 strong, was a magnificent fighting unit, but for all their qualities they were put to a tremendous test in and around the Le Mesnil crossroads. They were in action on D-Day and in some respects, even more so in the days to come. Many fell but no one crossed the ridge. They held it."

Photographer Sergeant D.A. Reynolds, National Archives of Canada, PA 130154.

During this very active and dangerous period, Canadian paratroopers were instrumental in assuring the protection and eventual withdrawal to the newly established beachhead of the invasion glider pilots, as well as downed Allied fighter and bomber pilots. The extensive pre-invasion training and recently gathered operational experience necessitated that these individuals were removed from the combat zone as quickly as possible so as to husband their special skills until the next mission. For the Allies, aircraft could be quickly replaced — trained pilots, however, could not.

Glider pilots being immediately evacuated to England.

Fatigue, the soldier's constant companion, is clearly evident in the faces of these Canadian paratroopers standing ready to oppose the inevitable German counter-attack. A Mills M-36 defensive grenade is in the foreground.

Courtesy of the 1 Canadian Parachute Battalion Association Archives.

In regard to 1 Canadian Parachute Battalion's performance on D-Day, Brigadier James Hill wrote, "they really put up a most tremendous performance on D-Day and as a result of their tremendous dash and enthusiasm they overcame their objectives, which were very sticky ones, with considerable ease." Hill always maintained a special affection for his Canadian wards. "They were the only Canadian troops," he explained to journalist and writer Brian Nolan in the post-war years, "entirely cut off from their own army. I felt responsible for their lives and welfare and that they were a long way from home. I took that very seriously, particularly in the fighting. It was very important that I looked after them and it paid tremendous dividends."

Courtesy of the 1 Canadian Parachute Battalion Association Archives.

Airborne medic W.S. Ducker tends to a wounded German Prisoner of War (PW) on D-Day. Two weeks later, on 19 June 1944, Ducker died of wounds.

Courtesy of the 1 Canadian Parachute Battalion Association Archives.

General Sir Richard Gale, Commander 6th British Airborne Division, during the Normandy Invasion. "I will always remember with gratitude," wrote General Gale in 1977, "those happy days when the 1st Canadian Parachute Battalion and I soldiered together. It was a long time ago but the memories are vivid today."

Photographer Sergeant Christie, IWM, Negative B 5352.

Captured! Private Jan de Vries recalls "the pilots took such evasive action on the run-in because of flak that it resulted in inaccurate drops and stretched out sticks." Lance Corporal H.R. Holloway was less diplomatic. He stated, "airplanes dropped us all over hell's half acre." The inevitable result was the capture of a number of paratroopers who landed far from their objectives in the midst of heavy German troop concentrations.

All photos: Courtesy of the 1 Canadian Parachute Battalion Association Archives.

In the minutes and hours following the drop, as well as the following few days, many French civilians, partisans, and in some cases children, in total disregard for their personal safety, were instrumental in providing information pertaining to German troop dispositions and movements. They also provided food and shelter, and in certain instances assisted in corralling isolated paratroopers. "C" Company reported that partisans were quite active. They noted, "one Frenchman in particular distinguished himself. Upon being given a red beret and a rifle he killed three German snipers."

Photographer Sergeant D.A. Reynolds, National Archives of Canada, PA 129045.

Photographer Sergeant D.A. Reynolds, National Archives of Canada, PA 130155.

Canadian and British paratroopers steal a brief pause in the battle, Normandy, France, 8 June 1944. "C" Company operating in the Varaville area also observed that "during this time the local inhabitants were of great assistance, the women dressing wounds and the men offering assistance in any way." Similarly, "B" Company commented that a woman had guided Lieutenant Norman Toseland and 30 men through marshes and an enemy minefield to help them reach their objective, the Robehomme Bridge.

Photographer Sergeant D.A. Reynolds, National Archives of Canada, PA 209701.

Once the local French population became aware that the invading Allied force was well-established, their exuberance and joy often hampered the tasks of the paratroopers. Corporal Dan Hartigan remembered one such incident on the morning of 6 June: "A large middle-aged French woman comes out of her house, and when she realizes we are invasion troops, she becomes ecstatic. She hugs and kisses us and wants us to come into her house for refreshments. On our polite refusal she agrees to take care of a jumper with a broken leg."

Not all interactions with the French population were so upbeat. Airborne photographer Sergeant D. R. Reynolds and Major Jeff Nicklin were greeted by an irritated elderly lady who had been roused from her sleep. "You are most welcome," she insisted, "but you make too much noise."

While some paratroopers could relax in a safe environment, others, such as Private Alexander Huton, were stranded for many days behind enemy lines, forcing them to survive on meagre rations that eventually ran out. Huton recalled that members of the resistance did everything in their power to assist them. "The Frenchmen," he said, "brought as much food as they could but it wouldn't go around and we were pretty hungry. They suggested killing their dog and eating it but we wouldn't let them. It was a swell pup. We would rather go hungry than kill it."

The German soldiers who fought against 1 Canadian Parachute Battalion were tenacious and took full advantage of the terrain. Enemy snipers continually engaged the Canadian paratroopers, making everyday life increasingly hazardous. Danger lurked everywhere and the airborne soldiers could never let their guard down, not even during temporary truces arranged to allow for the evacuation of the wounded. One incident stuck out in Corporal Dan Hartigan's memory: "Suddenly the two-wheeled wagon that he [Captain Hanson] had given to the German sergeant came around the gatehouse and through the passageway between it and the wagon house. With it came three or four walking enemy wounded and what appeared to be a healthy German sergeant.... Then, without rhyme, reason or warning, an enemy machine gunner at their trench system opened fire on their own wagon.... The reason for this strange behaviour still remains a puzzle."

Similarly, "B" Company CSM Johnny Kemp also witnessed the enemy's unpredictability. "When Toseland was injured he was going to take a prisoner," Kemp explained. "The young German was sitting whimpering asking for help. When Toseland went over to him he [the German] pulled out a handgun and shot Toseland in the belly. So we shot the German."

Boyd Anderson experienced a few close calls himself while hiding from a German combat patrol: "First they hit us with a grenade and then followed up with machine gun fire. It just seemed that it was not the day for MacPherson and me to leave the world. How the machine gun fire missed us, I will never know.... We found out later that some of Germany's crack troops were in this area. My experience with them so far had convinced me that they were good at their job."

Photographer Sergeant D.A. Reynolds, National Archives of Canada, PA 142269.

Fatigue is clearly evident in the eyes and facial appearance of "Spike and Lee" during the Normandy Campaign in France.

On two different occasions, Canadian paratroopers rescued downed Allied pilots. In this particular case, on 10 July, German anti-aircraft guns had hit a British Spitfire. The pilot crash-landed his plane near defensive positions occupied by "C" Company. To further complicate the situation the plane skidded, knocked down a fence, and finally stopped in a German minefield. Cows wandered into the minefield and set off a series of mines. Paratroopers carefully approached the aircraft and extracted the wounded pilot.

The second rescue mission took place during the week of 12–19 July. This time it involved retrieving an injured U.S. Thunderbolt pilot from the waters of the Orne River, near a 1 Canadian Parachute Battalion rest area. The pilot's mobility was restricted because of a broken leg. A British sergeant swam out to him and pulled him back to shore where Major Hanson, assisted by Sergeant Morgan and other Canadian paratroopers, pulled the pilot out of the water while under heavy machine-gun and mortar fire. Sergeant Morgan later received a Military Medal for his role in this rescue operation.

A tenacious foe. "The Germans," insisted Private Jan de Vries, "would lose a lot of men before giving up an attack." Members of 1 Canadian Parachute Battalion pose by destroyed German tanks in France.

A memorable welcome for a liberator. "No soldier involved could ask for more," Dan Hartigan later wrote of the invasion of Europe. "Exciting challenges, tests of ingenuity, matching of wits with a clever and dedicated enemy. More adventure in one night than most men live in a lifetime."

Courtesy of the 1 Canadian Parachute Battalion Association Archives.

Courtesy of the 1 Canadian Parachute Battalion Association Archives.

The reason for victory — the individual paratroopers. Dan Hartigan wrote, "the very threat of defeat evidently summoned from the distant reaches of their collective being an escalation of fortitude — 'a rising of courage.'... There was no question in anyone's mind that the objective not being taken was thinkable. That just wasn't an option."

Courtesy of the 1 Canadian Parachute Battalion Association Archives.

Courtesy of the 1 Canadian Parachute Battalion Association Archives.

Rudko, Bray, and Spud on the edge of a bomb

crater in Normandy, June 1944.

Paratrooper or partisan. The chaos of the battlefield quickly eroded the uniformity of garrison life.

Ted Kalicki and Lee experiment with alternate forms of transportation in Normandy.

Universal "Bren Gun" carriers mounting .50-calibre machine guns used to support the infantry during the breakout of the Normandy salient.

Protective cover was a constant concern, even when pulled out of the line. One paratrooper told the *Winnipeg Free Press* that there "must have been a mortar for every two Nazis." Jan de Vries felt that shelling "was probably the worst thing to have to live through."

Courtesy of the 1 Canadian Parachute Battalion Association Archives.

Courtesy of the 1 Canadian Parachute Battalion Association Archives.

Sergeant Evans and the remnants of 3 Platoon prepare for a "bath parade" in France on the occasion of being pulled out of the front lines, 4–20 July 1944, for the first time since the invasion.

Reinforcements for Normandy at the Bulford

Siding, England, 8 August 1944.

Photographer Lieutenant Ken Bell, National Archives of Canada, PA 162334.

Following the Normandy invasion and subsequent breakout, the Allied Senior Command invited Russian officers to tour the battlefields of the recent campaigns. Allied commanders and politicians considered this an important diplomatic initiative to demonstrate Allied commitment and sacrifice. This was deemed necessary because of the demands of the Russian dictator, Joseph Stalin, who had for years called for a second front to relieve the pressure on his beleaguered forces on the Eastern Front. Pictured is Major-General Gale showing a group of Russian officers (Lieutenant-Colonel Tamplin, Rear-Admiral Kharlamor, Major-General Sklearov, and Colonel Gorbatov) one of the Norman glider fields, 28 July 1944.

Photographer unknown, National Archives of Canada, PA 209709.

On 16 July 1944, General Bernard Montgomery presented medals and addressed paratroopers of various British airborne and parachute formations. "He has quite a soft spot for the 6th Airborne Division," commented Major Peter Griffin, "and [he] spoke to us at great length. He told us what an important job we'd done in securing the left flank of his beachhead and subsequent bridgehead."

Photographer Lieutenant M.M. Dean, National Archives of Canada, PA 193271.

Lance-Corporal Russell Geddes receives the Military Medal on 16 July 1944. By war's end, the Battalion members had earned a myriad of honours and awards, including one Victoria Cross, one Distinguished Service Order, one Officer of The Order of The British Empire, one Member of the Order of The British Empire, three Military Crosses, two Distinguished Conduct Medals, nine Military Medals, nineteen Mentioned in Dispatches, and an American Silver Star.

Courtesy of the 1 Canadian Parachute Battalion Association Archives.

Pulled from battle and en route to England, CSM J. Kemp and "B" Company HQ personnel in Ostend Belgium, September 1944.

Passing through Belgium.

Courtesy of the 1 Canadian Parachute Battalion Association Archives.

Photographer Lieutenant J. Smith, National Archives of Canada, PA 209708.

In Normandy, death and injury came in many forms — bad parachute landings, drowning due to the flooded countryside, small arms, mortar and artillery fire, booby traps and anti-personnel mines. Clearly, the Canadian paratroopers could never let their guard down. "We lost about six men from booby traps and mines," acknowledged CSM Johnny Kemp. "I think two were killed and four wounded. They were 'S' mines, or jumping mines. There were three prongs that stuck out of the ground. It was in a casing. When you stepped on it, it activated. When you took your foot off it, it jumped up about three feet and exploded. It was full of ball-bearing shot and could kill or wound anyone within a radius of fifty yards."

Despite being wounded, many paratroopers refused to be separated from their unit. Ross Munro, a Canadian war correspondent, was amazed at the incredible stamina of the paratroopers and the fact that the only thing that mattered was staying with their comrades. "The Canadian paratrooper," he reported, "showed toughness and there were only three cases of battle exhaustion during the entire battle. One wounded Canadian was evacuated to the beach, but went absent without leave and rejoined his unit at Le Mesnil despite his wounds."

Of the original 544 paratroopers dropped on 6 June, twenty-one were killed or died of wounds, nine were wounded, and eighty-four were captured. After it's first day in France the Battalion had lost roughly 25 percent of its personnel.

Upon their return to England, the unit spent September resting and refitting. Reinforcements were brought in from the 1 Canadian Parachute Training Battalion. Due to the heavy losses incurred during the Normandy Campaign, (83 killed or died of wounds, 187 wounded, 87 captured) the new Commanding Officer, Lieutenant-Colonel Jeff Nicklin, devised a rigorous training schedule that encompassed many training elements from the pre-D-Day period, as well as new material that was incorporated as a result of the lessons learned during the Normandy Campaign.

Gruelling physical training was once again emphasized, as was range work. Special attention was also placed on street-fighting courses given in the London and the Battersea areas. Other training requirements integrated into the rifle company training were: sniper school, platoon battle procedures, platoon level attacks on built-up areas, demolition, hand stripping of enemy weapons, identification of and working with booby traps, battle first aid, communications, specifically work with the 18, 38, and 68 sets and line telephony, German vehicle recognition, daylight reconnaissance for night occupation of defensive positions, defence of wooded areas, and use of 75 grenades to blow slit trenches. Evening training was instituted to ensure that the plethora of material could be covered and practised.

Photographer unknown, National Archives of Canada, PA 209736.

This paratrooper attempts to overcome the airborne's Achilles heel — mobility — by use of a bicycle. Pictured, at the reinforcement camp of 1 Canadian Parachute Battalion, is Private Tom Phelan, who was recovering from wounds suffered on 16 June at Le Mesnil.

Photographer unknown, National Archives of Canada, PA 204971.

Photographer Sergeant C.H. Lattion, National Archives of Canada, PA 191136.

A patrol from 1 Canadian Parachute Battalion prepares to leave friendly lines near Roy, Belgium, 13 January 1945. The Battalion officers recalled that "if there was no fighting going on, Brigadier Hill made sure there was patrolling. He wanted to impart the superiority of our troops — he never wanted the enemy to rest."

1 Canadian Parachute Battalion's activities in Belgium attracted the attention of Canadian press. *The Maple Leaf* newspaper for Canadian soldiers overseas reported that the Canadian "dare-devil airborne fighters are known as hell-damners." The article went on to describe the exploits of the "tough Canadian parachutists" and their 11–18 hour patrols in the Ardennes forest.

Photographer Sergeant Mike Lattion, National Archives of Canada, PA 130727.

C.W. Patterson in the Belgian Ardennes, January 1945. Private E.H. Jackson recalled, "conditions in the Ardennes were horrible. It was said to be the worst winter they had in many years and I believe it."

Courtesy of the 1 Canadian Parachute Battalion Association Archives.

Photographer T/5 J. Runyan, U.S. Signal Corps, Negative 7075.

CSM John Kemp and Sergeant Bill Murray ham it up for the camera, Ardennes, January 1945.

Courtesy of the 1 Canadian Parachute Battalion Association Archives.

Courtesy of the 1 Canadian Parachute Battalion Association Archives.

Paratroopers in the Ardennes, January 1945. 1 Canadian Parachute Battalion was the only Canadian unit to participate in the "Battle of the Bulge." The perception of the battle by most of the Battalion members, however, was summed up by Jan de Vries. He stated, "Every day, it seemed, we moved up to attack a village, were shelled a bit; then found that the Germans had left."

Unit signals personnel maintain a vigil, Holland, January 1945.

Courtesy of the 1 Canadian Parachute Battalion Association Archives.

The cost of war — nothing is sacred.

Courtesy of the 1 Canadian Parachute Battalion Association Archives.

A. Bruno and Jan de Vries in Buggenum, Holland, February 1945. "To me," reminisced Private de Vries, "it was a confusing time."

Unit personnel at Buggenum, on the Maas River in Holland, February 1945.

D. Morrison and Herb Fulcher capture their time at Haelen, Maas River, Holland, on film, 2 February 1945. The leather jerkins were official issue.

One must wonder if this photograph prompted Field Marshal Montgomery to later write in regard to the paratrooper "What manner of men are these who wear the maroon beret.... Every man an Emperor." Field expedient bath in Holland, 1945.

The integral fire support of the Battalion's mortar platoon was a critical component of its ability to conduct both defensive and offensive operations.

Courtesy of the 1 Canadian Parachute Battalion Association Archives.

Courtesy of the 1 Canadian Parachute Battalion Association Archives.

Captain John Madden supervises the loading of a Bren Gun carrier, on 24 March 1945, in preparation for *Operation Varsity*. Sergeant Andy Anderson recalled, "I have a clear memory that when I finally reached the Battalion, and was assigned to 'B' Company, it was a revelation to serve officers, who were young and fit, and who had all the required skills for leadership. This was a far cry from the experience I had with another Service, and going back to the days in the Militia."

Courtesy of the 1 Canadian Parachute Battalion Association Archives.

Courtesy of the 1 Canadian Parachute Battalion Association Archives.

Sergeant W.H.C. Fitzsimons of the Vickers Platoon checks the load of a Hamilcar glider in preparation for the Rhine Crossing.

C-47 Dakotas assigned to carry 3 Parachute Brigade line up in England in preparation for *Operation Varsity*, 24 March 1945.

Courtesy of the 1 Canadian Parachute Battalion Association Archives.

Courtesy of the 1 Canadian Parachute Battalion Association Archives.

Photographer Lieutenant C.H. Richer, National Archives of Canada, PA 162036.

Major-General E.L. Bols, GOC 6 Airborne Division, delivering a briefing to assembled airborne officers at a transit camp near Ipswick, prior to Operation Varsity, on 22 March 1945. He stated: "Well gentlemen, you'll be glad to know that this time we're not going to be dropped down as a carrot held out for the ground forces. This time the Army and Navy are going to storm across the Rhine, and just when they've gained Jerry's attention — bingo! We drop down behind him. The trouble is that the only dropping zones in the vicinity are fairly well-packed with 20 millimetre ack-ack gun and machine-gun posts. That means we'll have to fight for our landing and dropping zones. As a matter of fact, we'll have a helluva fight when we first get down. If things go according to plan with the Second Army, we'll be fighting like stink for the first day. However, things never go according to plan, so we'll be ready to fight it out for 48 hours. This operation will be real teamwork. Under my command will be the First Canadian Paratroop Battalion, which will drop on this high, wooded feature here. The American air-borne division to the south of us and ourselves make up a corps under the command of the American General Ridgway, for whom I have great regard and affection. He's a helluva nice soldier. We operate under the command of Field Marshal Montgomery, and over us all is Ike Eisenhower. That, gentlemen, is a real allied team, and should make the sparks fly. Unless I miss my guess the initial tough fighting should break the crust of the remaining good troops the enemy has against us, and then I think we'll swarm out all over Germany."

After the briefing, Major-General Bols exchanges a few pleasantries with British airborne officers and Lieutenant-Colonel Jeff Nicklin, CO of 1 Canadian Parachute Battalion. Two days later, Nicklin was killed in the airborne assault during the crossing of the Rhine River.

Photographer Sergeant Christie, IWM, H 41536.

Courtesy of the 1 Canadian Parachute Battalion Association Archives.

Sergeant Andy Anderson felt that "our Battalion and Brigade had the most superb leadership in the Officer Corps.... [W]ith only one exception, all the officers I served with were young, fit and aggressive, but they had all the skills of leadership that earned your support."

Pictured are: (front row) Jack Davies, Pete Isling, Sam McGowan, Jack Burnett (back row) Captain Vic Fleming, Major Clay Fuller. Ironically, the OC, Major Fuller, never flew in the aircraft named after him. Canadian headquarters notified his CO that Fuller had served five years overseas and, therefore, was to be repatriated to Canada. Despite Fuller's protests, he was left out of battle.

Waiting for the order to emplane. Sergeant Andy Anderson recalled, "If ever a fighting unit was ready for anything, this had to be it. My personal concern is that I can measure up, and not let anyone down."

Courtesy of the 1 Canadian Parachute Battalion Association Archives.

Nothing to chance! Final check of equipment and fitting of parachutes on 24 March 1945.

Courtesy of the 1 Canadian Parachute Battalion Association Archives.

  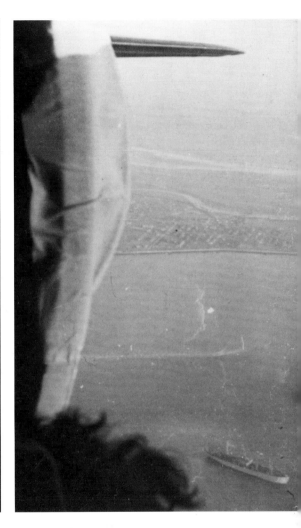

En route to the Battalion's final combat jump — the Crossing of the Rhine, 24 March 1945. Different veterans remembered the historic moment in different ways. Lieutenant-Colonel Eadie recalled that "The crew chief had hollered, 'Stand in the door' and all jumpers were crowding to the exit. The batman tapped the second in command on the shoulder and said, 'What a wonderful day out there, we should have gone fishing.' What a wonderful alternative it would have been but it was to late to even consider it. Green light — GO!!!"

Sergeant Andy Anderson reminisced, "Looking out the window briefly before 'Stand Up,' my impression was of a very wide 'lake.' I have no idea what I expected, but the river was massive, cold and uninviting.... Within seconds someone hollered the customary 'stand up and hook up.'"

A formation of C-47 Dakota aircraft ferrying Allied airborne forces during *Operation Varsity*, the crossing of the Rhine River, 24 March 1945. "The Yank aircraft did a hell of a job for us," asserted the Battalion Commanding Officer. "I have never been on a better drop, not training or operational." Private Jan de Vries stated, "We went out in a tight formation; the pilots took no evasive action." Private A.H. Carignan recalled, "The flight over was uneventful, the NCOs inspired confidence."

Photographer Ken Bell, National Archives of Canada, PA 137342.

Courtesy of the 1 Canadian Parachute Battalion Association Archives.

Glider force en route to the Reich. Major Fraser Eadie told reporters after the battle, "We met no opposition until we were right over the dropping zone. The air cover was wonderful, and as far as we know only two of our tow planes were shot down from the ground."

No turning back. Paratroopers of 1 Canadian Parachute Battalion en route to Germany during *Operation Varsity*, 24 March 1945. "It was a gorgeous morning," reminisced Dan Hartigan, "one of the most beautiful days I've ever experienced."

Courtesy of the 1 Canadian Parachute Battalion Association Archives.

Courtesy of the 1 Canadian Parachute Battalion Association Archives.

Private M. Zakaluk recounted his experience: "My turn to leave the aircraft! I am out, chute opened, cascading down. What are all these bees doing at 300–400 feet in the month of March? Buzzing all around me!! I can't see them, but I can hear them. A little early to be buzzing around at these heights. Hey! These guys are shooting at me!! I made a landing within a few seconds. I notice that these killer bees are down here too!"

Courtesy of the 1 Canadian Parachute Battalion Association Archives.

Private Jan de Vries remembered, "I heard bullets going by and looked up to see bullet holes in my chute. My thoughts were to get down fast."

Courtesy of the 1 Canadian Parachute Battalion Association Archives.

Courtesy of the 1 Canadian Parachute Battalion Association Archives.

Many did not make a safe landing and became casualties before hitting the ground or while hung-up in the trees. Fraser Eadie said of the resistance on the DZ, "It was hot!"

Courtesy of the 1 Canadian Parachute Battalion Association Archives.

Suicide wood.

The Rhine DZ (*Operation Varsity*), 24 March 1945. The price paid for the flat piece of earth is still evident in the background.

The unsecured DZ. Major Richard Hilborn told reporters after the battle, "it was real flat-out fighting until about noon." Fraser Eadie was more direct. He simply acknowledged that it was "two hours of real killing."

Courtesy of the 1 Canadian Parachute Battalion Association Archives.

Courtesy of the 1 Canadian Parachute Battalion Association Archives.

Courtesy of the 1 Canadian Parachute Battalion Association Archives.

This shot was taken at approximately 1100 hours and shows gliders coming in to land on the Battalion's DZ. The nearest glider had just landed and carried the Mortar Platoon's carrier and trailer, which contained spare mortar tubes and ammunition.

The glider fields of the Rhine River.

Wrecked gliders on the Landing Zone (LZ), *Operation Varsity*.

Photographer Lieutenant C.H. Richer, National Archives of Canada, PA 205203.

Photographer Sergeant Christie, IWM, BU 2283.

The gliders that landed intact with their precious cargo were quickly emptied. The Normandy drop almost ten months earlier had revealed many airborne planning deficiencies. These were now addressed. For the Rhine drop, the paratroopers were provided with additional vehicles and artillery that proved vital for their survival in the event that the link-up with the ground force was delayed.

Penetrating the Reich. Airborne troops move along the edge of the Drop Zone following the end of German resistance during *Operation Varsity*. Sergeant Anderson eloquently captured the sentiments of most. He stated, "at the conclusion of the first day, I think it would be fair comment to suggest that everyone was both exhausted and personally pleased to have survived. Exhaustion came from the effects, not only of the 'fighting' but the tension that has been building for days. There was also some feeling that the success of the mission perhaps did in fact mean a rapid end to the war."

Courtesy of the 1 Canadian Parachute Battalion Association Archives.

Dug-in on the edge of the DZ.

Courtesy of the 1 Canadian Parachute Battalion Association Archives.

A lone paratrooper stands beside a British Airspeed Horsa Troop Glider on the LZ near Wesel, Germany, 24 March 1945.

Paratroopers on the DZ. Private A.H. Carignan recalled the anxieties and pressures prior to the battle: "My fears and apprehensions may have been a bit falsely eased by the fact that only a few episodes of artillery, mortar and small arms fire were encountered in Belgium and Holland. The confidence inspired by our NCOs and the roughly half of the ORs who had survived Normandy were great for morale. Of course, only an idiot or a maniac would have no fear or doubt of jumping onto enemy held objectives, but the fact that we green horns had been able to not only keep up but in many cases outperform some of those experienced chaps did give us confidence that we would not let down our comrades. Most men, if honestly answering, 'what was your greatest fear?' will tell you that it was the fear that one might not fulfil the expectations of his comrades under extreme duress. That's why the bonds between men (or women) who have endured common hardship and losses are so strong."

An airborne Bren gunner and PIAT anti-tank team remain vigilant on the edge of the woods skirting the DZ, 24 March 1945.

Courtesy of the 1 Canadian Parachute Battalion Association Archives.

Paratroopers at their RV, approximately two miles east of the Rhine, 24 March 1945. Major Hilborn observed, "it was a wonderful show. It was individual fighting in the first stages until we got organized and the boys did a terrific job."

Courtesy of the 1 Canadian Parachute Battalion Association Archives.

"After the Battle." Sid Carignan, Bob Surtee, and Morley White (left to right) from 1 Section, 1 Platoon, "A" Company, share a shell scrape on the edge of the DZ during *Operation Varsity*.

Courtesy of the 1 Canadian Parachute Battalion Association Archives.

German prisoners captured on the Battalion's objective being herded into a temporary compound, 24 March 1945.

Photographer unknown, National Archives of Canada, PA 16030.

Courtesy of the 1 Canadian Parachute Battalion Association Archives.

German prisoners being marched into internment. One Canadian paratrooper commented that "the Red Beret always speaks for itself, and the German troops seem to show respect."

Courtesy of the 1 Canadian Parachute Battalion Association Archives.

Respected foes — captured young German paratroopers.

Stealth and guile, as well as speed and efficient use of available firepower, were all critical tenets of airborne warfare that enabled the paratroopers to repeatedly destroy enemy troops who were often numerically superior and better equipped.

A Sherman "Firefly" and M3 Halftrack, representing the first reconnaissance elements of the Fifteenth Scottish Division, reach 1 Canadian Parachute Battalion, late 24 March 1945. Sergeant Anderson later recalled, "Sure enough, at about 1630 hours, we heard the unmistakable sound of tracked vehicles coming up the road from the direction of the river. Within minutes, there was the start of some cheering, as Recce vehicles followed by Bren Gun Carriers and tanks move into sight. These were the leading elements of the British Fifteenth Scottish Division."

Courtesy of the 1 Canadian Parachute Battalion Association Archives.

Photographer Lieutenant C.H. Richer, National Archives of Canada, PA 145734.

Photographer Lieutenant C.H. Richer, National Archives of Canada, PA 137349.

The main body of the Fifteenth Scottish Division linked up with the Canadian paratroopers at approximately 0430 hours, 25 March 1945, Bergerfurth Wald, Germany. Private F.M. Estok greets Lieutenant J.E. Foley.

Photographer Lieutenant C.H. Richer, National Archives of Canada, PA 180401.

Photographer Lieutenant C.H. Richer, National Archives of Canada, PA 151491.

After the battle. Paratroopers prepare their first warm food (chicken and chips) in over 24 hours. CSM J.M. Kemp, Lieutenant A.J. Esling, Captain S. McGowan, Lieutenant V.E. Fleming and (in rear) Private W.B. White and Private J. Pasco.

After the battle. Corporal C.J. Scott (brushing teeth) and Private R.D. Amaolo (shaving) utilize a pause in the war to conduct personal ablutions, Bergerfurth Wald, 25 March 1945.

Photographer Lieutenant C.H. Richer, National Archives of Canada, PA 162024.

A respite after the battle. This unidentified paratrooper reflects the strength of youth supported by confidence. Private Jan de Vries recalled, "We had a feeling that whatever was required, we could do."

The inevitable consequence of war. 1 Canadian Parachute Battalion personnel gather up their dead, 24 March 1945.

Courtesy of the 1 Canadian Parachute Battalion Association Archives.

Courtesy of the 1 Canadian Parachute Battalion Association Archives.

Brigadier James Hill (right) after the battle. Fraser Eadie, the newly appointed CO of 1 Canadian Parachute Battalion stated, "the operation was extremely well carried out based on a simple plan that the Brigadier had set up." The Brigadier himself was loved by his Canadian paratroopers. Veterans describe him as "a soldier's soldier" and as "an icon to each and every man" who served in the unit. Sergeant Andy Anderson explained, "In line of march and in any attack, you could always find the Brigadier at your elbow. His courage and leadership inspired us." Many veterans recalled his calm manner and understated "Come along Chaps nothing to worry about" as he gathered up an ad hoc force of paratroopers to conduct a counter-attack.

Photographer Lieutenant C.H. Richer, National Archives of Canada, PA 137351.

Courtesy of the 1 Canadian Parachute Battalion Association Archives.

The "morning after." Brewing up prior to commencing the advance into the heart of the Reich.

Courtesy of the 1 Canadian Parachute Battalion Association Archives.

The battle won, the pursuit into the heart of the Reich now awaited the weary paratroopers. But the indomitable airborne spirit always prevailed. One Canadian paratrooper captured its essence when he encouraged his mates by simply stating, "Come on, lets get this over with."

Cutting into the Reich. The enemy's exposed jugular was now evident and the pursuit to destroy Germany's remaining military forces was pursued relentlessly. As a result, the next engagement was sought even before the dead from the just-finished battle were recovered.

Photographer Captain Malindine, IWM, BU 2397.

Photographer Captain Malindine, IWM, BU 2395.

Major-General Bols and Brigadier Hill discuss the penetration of the Reich. They received direction, from Prime Minister Churchill himself, to beat the Russians to the Baltic Sea.

The thrust into the Reich. 3 Parachute Brigade, in keeping with the motto of the Sixth Airborne Division, "Go to it!", commenced its advance across Germany to the Baltic with the Third Tank Battalion Scots Guards under command.

Courtesy of the 1 Canadian Parachute Battalion Association Archives.

Courtesy of the 1 Canadian Parachute Battalion Association Archives.

Fulfilment of a prophecy — Canadian paratroopers begin to dismantle the Reich. On 17 August 1942, *Globe and Mail* journalist Sydney Gruson had reported on the creation of a Canadian parachute unit. He wrote that its inception "seemed to hint that some day in the future Canadian fighting men would strike out of the sky onto the ground at the enemy along with the masses of Canadian men and machines now ready for the offensive. That is a hope shared by the men summed up best, perhaps by the acting Regimental Sergeant-Major (RSM), Ash Clifton, who said, 'Just let me drop in at any Nazi military headquarters after I've learned to jump, armed with a few grenades and a tommy gun, Mister, that would be sufficient.'"

Courtesy of the 1 Canadian Parachute Battalion Association Archives.

Courtesy of the 1 Canadian Parachute Battalion Association Archives.

Courtesy of the 1 Canadian Parachute Battalion Association Archives.

Courtesy of the 1 Canadian Parachute Battalion Association Archives.

Despite the gruelling pace, maintenance of equipment was essential, especially with weapons such as the unit's 81mm mortars, which provided integral indirect fire support. The mortar was a very effective, yet universally despised weapon. Most veterans agree that shelling "was probably the worst thing to have to live through." Private Jan de Vries confessed, "After a barrage let up I used to feel guilty that during a barrage I prayed that the shells would fall somewhere else, knowing that it meant on someone else."

Into the heart of the Reich. Paratroopers advance relentlessly to the Baltic Sea. One veteran recalled that "It was a rotation of walk, ride on tanks, ride on trucks and then the cycle would start again." Private Jan de Vries commented, "My impression was that you knew it was over and so did they. Enemy action became more of a nuisance than anything else."

Courtesy of the 1 Canadian Parachute Battalion Association Archives.

Courtesy of the 1 Canadian Parachute Battalion Association Archives.

Courtesy of the 1 Canadian Parachute Battalion Association Archives.

The relentless pursuit. Exhausted paratroopers take a much needed break. Brigadier Hill noted that all the physical training conducted in England "gave us an invaluable asset — endurance."

Photographer Lieutenant C.H. Richer, National Archives of Canada, PA 209710

The ingenuity of the paratroopers never failed to surface. Any device useful to speed up the advance was pressed into service. These paratroopers are on the move from Bergerfarth Wald to Lembeck, 28 March 1945.

Courtesy of the 1 Canadian Parachute Battalion Association Archives.

The quickness of the advance did have a price. "Often times," recalled Lieutenant-Colonel Eadie, "there was no time to fully brief everyone. The poor soldiers — they would learn of things at the last minute with normally an 'up on your feet, let's go, we're attacking the town." Private Del Parlee agreed. "Troops lacked information," he stated. "You just didn't know what was going on. You were just told to do something — often even the officers didn't know."

Courtesy of the 1 Canadian Parachute Battalion Association Archives.

Photographer Lieutenant C.H. Richer, National Archives of Canada, PA 191134

Race to the sea. British Prime Minister Churchill gave his senior commanders firm direction to beat the Russians to the Baltic. Lieutenant Tucker affirmed that he personally took the message from Brigade headquarters that "we were to proceed to the Baltic by any means we could and not to let the Russians over-run us." The Brigade signallers also stated, he added, that the message was sent directly from London and did not go through the normal military chain of command. Not surprisingly, tanks were quickly converted to taxis.

The frenzied pace of the advance prompted Private E.H. Jackson to recall, "Again we are mounted on decks of tanks, the pace is very fast. We are running through towns and villages too fast to recollect. Where we are stopped with shooting, the tanks merely level the opposition, in most cases there is no need to dismount the troops. Everything is speed and shoot anything that gets in the way."

"The routine," explained Private E.H. Jackson, "is advance as far as possible for the day, dig in for the night and hold. We are making about 15 miles per day, rotating with other Companies and Platoons for the Point." Jan de Vries captured the sentiment of most soldiers. "It struck me," he remembered, "that having always been 'on point' so to speak very little information reached us. I never knew just where Battalion headquarters was or the other Battalion companies. It was always vaguely 'over there somewhere.'"

One veteran recalled "the trek across Germany was a blur — attack some towns and villages (I was missed by a German bazooka in one place), ride on tanks one day, ride on trucks another."

Photographer unknown, IWM, BU 3836.

The Germans were masters at delaying operations. Therefore, in order to maintain a rapid rate of advance to continually press the enemy's rear guard, yet minimize the deadly effects of sniper fire or simply harassing fire, paratroopers set fire to underbrush, flanking the axis of advance to create a natural and very thick smoke screen. Follow-on units were responsible for mopping up any by-passed resistance.

Photographer Lieutenant C.H. Richer, National Archives of Canada, PA 142610.

The years of training and combat were quickly evident. Sergeant Andy Anderson asserted, "Looking at the Battalion lined up, from a distance, it strikes me that perhaps this unit is at its very peak of performance. They look good, they are tough, all battle-stained, all very young and physically in the best form ever. I strongly suspect that at this moment, there is not another unit in any Army that could compare with these men on any basis. With some regret it strikes me that never again may it be possible to put together a unit like this, from all parts of Canada, sharing so much. There is an aura of pride coming from each man which is too difficult to describe."

Photographer Lieutenant C.H. Richer, National Archives of Canada, PA 114595.

P.L. Johnson and Sergeant D.R. Fairborn with a PIAT gun in Lembeck, Germany, 29 March 1945.

The consequences of total war: Coesfeld after the advance, 30 March 1945.

Photographer Lieutenant C.H. Richer, National Archives of Canada, PA 205202.

Photographer Lieutenant C.H. Richer, National Archives of Canada, PA 137325.

Private R.A. Boicey cleans his pistol during a pause in the advance in Lembeck, Germany, 29 March 1945.

Privates M.C. Ballance and R.S. Phillips fry eggs on the exhaust of a Churchill tank, Wiedensahl, Germany, 1 April 1945.

Photographer Lieutenant C.H. Richer, National Archives of Canada, PA 145971.

The inevitable destruction of towns and cities across Germany followed in the wake of continued resistance.

Courtesy of the 1 Canadian Parachute Battalion Association Archives.

The Battalion moves through Greven, Germany, 5 April 1945, after a bitter fight. "I guess our scrap to get Greven northwest of Munster was it," stated the CO to a *Globe and Mail* reporter. "We moved up 25 miles in tanks and the town was in a hell of a mess. There was a lot of confusion from shells and smoke and explosions and those guys were retreating and didn't know which were our troops and which were theirs. I whipped a company into Greven and we had to go through and around ammunition dumps which were blowing up. The Germans were retreating so we sent in three platoons with some German speaking personnel. They shook the hell out of the Jerries. It was the most beautiful job of killing I ever saw: really good. I guess you'd say that was 'A' Company's day."

Courtesy of the 1 Canadian Parachute Battalion Association Archives.

Photographer Lieutenant C.H. Richer, National Archives of Canada, PA 162853.

Masters of improvisation. Members of 1 Canadian Parachute Battalion utilize a gas railway buggy for transportation in Greven.

Members of 1 Canadian Parachute Battalion continue the advance from Greven, Germany, on bicycles, 5 April 1945.

Photographer Lieutenant C.H. Richer, National Archives of Canada, PA 205204.

Photographer Lieutenant C.H. Richer, National Archives of Canada, PA 205205.

The relentless advance continues. 1 Canadian Parachute Battalion in the village of Luthe, Germany, 8 April 1945.

"I suspect," mused Private E.H. Jackson, "that our general appearance, the Red Berets, the camouflage jackets, and the look of our tired men, unshaven, is enough to frighten most people who may have heard stories about the 'Paratroops' being ruthless."

Courtesy of the 1 Canadian Parachute Battalion Association Archives.

Courtesy of the 1 Canadian Parachute Battalion Association Archives.

1 Canadian Parachute Battalion Mortar Platoon personnel preparing for action in Germany, April 1945.

Courtesy of the 1 Canadian Parachute Battalion Association Archives.

Courtesy of the 1 Canadian Parachute Battalion Association Archives.

Canadian paratrooper with a confiscated German sporting rifle.

The carnage of war. (On the advance from Riestedt to Hansteadt to Uelzen.)

Courtesy of the 1 Canadian Parachute Battalion Association Archives.

Photographer Lieutenant. C.H. Richer, National Archives of Canada, PA 130330.

The speed of the advance necessitated that all possible means of transportation be "requisitioned." Captured German vehicles were quickly used to carry troops and push supplies and rations forward.

Photographer Lieutenant Charlie H. Richer, National Archives of Canada, PA 211200.

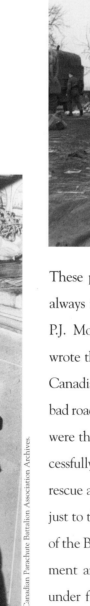

Courtesy of the 1 Canadian Parachute Battalion Association Archives.

These paratroopers steal a few moments of sleep — something that is always in short supply. In a letter dated 9 April 1945 to the Honourable P.J. Montague, Canadian Military Headquarters, Brigadier James Hill wrote that the pace of pursuit was gruelling. He praised the efforts of the Canadian parachutists and recounted "having marched 20 miles over very bad roads the day before, they marched a further 14 yesterday morning and were then called on to put in an assault on a small village. This they successfully did. Meanwhile, an S.O.S. had been sent out for them to try and rescue a small Recce detachment which was holding an important bridge just to the South of Hanover and in order to do this the leading company of the Battalion doubled pretty well non-stop for two miles with full equipment and stormed the bridge over an extremely open piece of ground under fire from three or four German S.P. [self-propelled] guns without turning a hair. They got the bridge intact, but the Recce Regiment unfortunately had been unable to hold out."

Lieutenant-Colonel Fraser Eadie inspects the Battalion, 24 April 1945, in Kolkhagen, Germany, in accordance with Brigadier Hill's insistence on maintaining order and discipline regardless of the surroundings. With the war practically won, a return to a more disciplined deportment took on a higher priority.

Courtesy of the 1 Canadian Parachute Battalion Association Archives.

Corporal F.G. Topham and Private A. Pakulak pose in Kolkhagen, Germany, April 1945. Corporal Topham won the Victoria Cross for his actions during *Operation Varsity*, specifically the battle for the DZ on 24 March. Despite heavy enemy fire, he repeatedly risked his life to evacuate wounded personnel and continued to do so even after he himself became wounded.

Photographer Lieutenant C.H. Richer, National Archives of Canada, PA 209735.

Lieutenant-Colonel Fraser Eadie, CO (left), and Major S.C. (Stan) Waters, OC "B" Company (right) discuss matters on 25 April 1945, in Kolkhagen, Germany. Major Waters came to 1 Canadian Parachute Battalion just prior to *Operation Varsity*. He served with the First Special Service Force (FSSF) up until its disbandment in December 1944. In the post-war years he wrote, "As one of the more battle experienced officers in the unit (having been in combat operations since August 1942), I felt that an important yet somewhat intangible aspect relates to the spirit, the physical energy, the aggressiveness and the courage of the officers and men in the unit. When I took command of "B" Company after the jump across the Rhine, I met them for the first time, my own spirits soared because I quickly sensed that here was a small combat unit that was ready to fight! Few know how difficult combat leadership in the infantry can be if the troops are not properly trained and physically and mentally ready. The superb state of mind, the high standards of fitness and training made my combat tour with "B" Company a relatively easy and memorable duty. I don't believe the history really captures this remarkable and rare characteristic of an outstanding combat unit — it was ready to fight!"

CQMS H.I. Smith from 1 Canadian Parachute Battalion, sporting an American M1 A1 .30-calibre carbine with metal folding stock and sheepskin coat, Germany, April 1945.

Courtesy of the 1 Canadian Parachute Battalion Association Archives.

1 Canadian Parachute Battalion awaiting its turn to cross the Elbe River, April 1945.

Courtesy of the 1 Canadian Parachute Battalion Association Archives.

Panoramic view of the war-scarred banks of the Elbe River, April 1945.

Courtesy of the 1 Canadian Parachute Battalion Association Archives.

The Battalion crossing the Elbe River on a pontoon bridge.

Courtesy of the 1 Canadian Parachute Battalion Association Archives.

"One thing is emerging," wrote Private E.H. Jackson, "from prisoners we are taking, and units we have overrun, the war seems to be closing fast, at least in our front." German prisoners near Wittenburg, Germany, May 1945.

One paratrooper recalled, "Prisoners are becoming a headache. We have no facilities, and we can't spare men to guard them or escort them to whatever rear we might have. So we try and keep them with us, they can dig trenches, carry some of the heavy gear, until we find some way to turn them over to another unit. In a quiet moment looking at perhaps fifty prisoners, it suddenly occurs to me that the age is perhaps 15 years, the kids have tears in their eyes. It is hard to convince some of them that they are not being asked to dig graves for themselves."

A vanquished army — the collapse of the Reich, May 1945. The 1 Canadian Parachute Battalion diary entry for 2 May 1945 provides a glimpse of the German desperation. It reads, "In a wood at Lutzow just before the refuelling point, we came across a German workshop detachment, numbering some 3,000, who had had orders to surrender. The confusion was indescribable in that wood. German civilian women, men and children were there, with the troops, and when the troops were lined up three deep on the road, they had their wives and children with them on the trek back to P.W. cages. This was because the rumour was ripe that the Russian Army was only nine miles away. The civilians and soldiers were terrified of the Russians and wanted to be taken by us."

The collapse of the German Army was also evident in the equipment that lay abandoned throughout the advance. Here a dreaded Nebelwerfer (15 cm rocket launcher), no longer terrorizes Allied soldiers. This weapon fired a group of six projectiles that created a nerve-shattering noise while in flight.

Courtesy of the 1 Canadian Parachute Battalion Association Archives.

Courtesy of the 1 Canadian Parachute Battalion Association Archives.

The feared, but well-respected 88mm anti-aircraft gun. It also proved to be, arguably, the best anti-armour weapon of the war.

Courtesy of the 1 Canadian Parachute Battalion Association Archives.

Courtesy of the 1 Canadian Parachute Battalion Association Archives.

Paratroopers pose with abandoned German tank destroyers.

Courtesy of the 1 Canadian Parachute Battalion Association Archives.

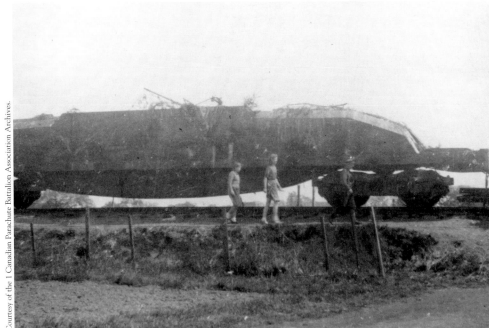

Courtesy of the 1 Canadian Parachute Battalion Association Archives.

Abandoned railway gun.

Desperate times call for desperate measures — an improvised German Armoured Fighting Vehicle (AFV) captured by the advancing paratroopers in the village of Brelingen. The AFV was actually only a small car with thin gauge metal used to give it the outline of a tank. It was incapable of stopping small arms munitions. Nonetheless, QM stores personnel used the vehicle for transport. Shown are Lieutenant W.B. Howard on the hull and RQMS J.S. Hull in the turret.

Photographer Lieutenant C.H. Richer, National Archives of Canada, PA 115483.

PART VI

OCCUPATION AND THE END OF THE CRUSADE

Photographer Lieutenant C.H. Richer, National Archives of Canada, PA150930.

West meets East. Link-up with the Soviets at Wismar on the Baltic Sea, 2 May 1945. "This bloody war is over!" was Private E. H. Jackson's immediate impression. Jerry McFadden, the OC of Headquarters Company, wrote his wife, "Well, its over! We ran out of Germans and ran into the Russians. May 2, 1945 was the last day of the war as far as we were concerned."

Sergeant C.M.G. Lattion talks with a Russian captain and the female driver for Field Marshal Rokossovsky at Wismar, Germany, 2 May 1945. The 1 Canadian Parachute Battalion War Diary account of the initial meeting between the Soviets and the Canadians was quite low-key. The diarist wrote: "On the night of 2 May, a Russian officer arrived in a jeep, with his driver. It was quite unofficial since he had no idea that we were in Wismar until he came to our barrier. He had come far in advance of his own columns, and was quite put out to find us sitting on what was the Russians' ultimate objective."

Courtesy of the 1 Canadian Parachute Battalion Association Archives.

Photographer Sergeant Oakes, IWM, Bu 5242.

The Battalion's ethnic mosaic paid great dividends. Many of the Canadian paratroopers were of European descent and still spoke their mother tongue. This was particularly useful when the paratroopers had to deal with their Russian counterparts in Wismar.

The Russians made a lasting impression on the paratroopers. "My first reaction," recalled Sergeant Andy Anderson, "was that they were the hardest looking bunch of toughs I had ever seen."

Courtesy of the 1 Canadian Parachute Battalion Association Archives.

Private Jan de Vries felt, "the Russians were fearless, but they were thoughtless of life. They appeared to believe that human life was dispensable."

Another veteran stated, "on the surface at least,

they seemed more like an enemy than an ally."

Courtesy of the 1 Canadian Parachute Battalion Association Archives.

Members of 1 Canadian Parachute Battalion (Scott, Sutherland, Peerless) with three Soviet airmen at Wismar, Germany, May 1945.

Courtesy of the 1 Canadian Parachute Battalion Association Archives.

Former German airfield in Wismar.

Courtesy of the 1 Canadian Parachute Battalion Association Archives.

Members of 1 Canadian Parachute Battalion (Laplante and Bill Benzak) pose with captured German aircraft, Wismar, May 1945.

"Winnie" poses in a captured German Focke Wulf Fw. 190 fighter aircraft, Wismar, May 1945.

Courtesy of the 1 Canadian Parachute Battalion Association Archives.

Natural curiosity. Harry Dzeoba checks out a German one-man glider at the Wismar airfield, May 1945. Sergeant A.N. Stammers believed that "The parachute battalion got the more adventurous type, those who wanted to get away from the hum-drum, those looking for a little more excitement, those with the attitude, 'let's give it a go!'"

Courtesy of the 1 Canadian Parachute Battalion Association Archives.

Members of 1 Canadian Parachute Battalion pose in front of a Junker Ju. 188 aircraft, in Wismar, May 1945. The camaraderie is clearly evident. "The short three years with the Parachute Battalion," insisted Sergeant Andy Anderson, "remains as the time I had the greatest pride and passion for what we were doing, and what we had achieved."

Courtesy of the 1 Canadian Parachute Battalion Association Archives.

An unidentified paratrooper in the cockpit of a Focke Wulf Fw. 190, Wismar, May 1945. The battalion had reached the end of the road. For many their reason for joining was now fulfilled. "I guess the main reason that I joined the paratroopers," insisted Private Harold Croft, "was to get overseas.... [It] sounded very exciting." Sergeant Appleton agreed: "I thought it would be a good unit with lots of excitement and action." And Corporal Grimes said, "I figured this unit offered plenty of different kinds of action." Similarly, Sergeant Peppard said, "I guess we all want to get some action." In the end, they all received what they wanted.

Courtesy of the 1 Canadian Parachute Battalion Association Archives.

Photographer Lieutenant C.H. Richer, National Archives of Canada, PA 204961.

Wishful thinking. However, the photo also captures the enduring sense of humour of the average soldier. In the post-war period Lieutenant-Colonel Fraser Eadie lamented that "Unfortunately, many writers have either misread or chose to neglect the very heart of what kept the average foot soldier going against seemingly insurmountable odds. Canadian ingenuity and a tremendous sense of humour, without which Canada's civilian soldier would never have been able to successfully accomplish the many tasks assigned to them."

Privates G.L. Wetherup and K.D. Wolfe from 1 Canadian Parachute Battalion stand guard over the Reichbank at Wismar, 7 May 1945.

Brigadier James Hill being presented the American Silver Star by General Matthew Ridgway, Commander XVIII Airborne Corps, somewhere in Germany, May 1945. Field Marshal Montgomery, Commander, Twenty-first Army Group, looks on.

Courtesy of the 1 Canadian Parachute Battalion Association Archives.

Lieutenant-Colonel Fraser Eadie receiving the American Silver Star somewhere in Germany, May 1945.

Courtesy of the 1 Canadian Parachute Battalion Association Archives.

Lieutenant-Colonel Fraser Eadie, standing in front of his Battalion Headquarters, proudly displays his American Silver Star, 20 May 1945, Wismar, Germany. Eadie would later write, "I shall ever remember, with great pride and affection, the energy and spirit of Canada's first paratroopers, who forged a proud legacy on the battlefields of Europe during World War II. An unprecedented level of physical fitness, an unrivalled skill-at-arms, and an unparalleled sense of self-confidence characterized the early airborne soldier. These paratroopers became the first Canadian troops to storm Hitler's Fortress Europe on D-Day. By war's end they had penetrated deeper into the Reich than any other Canadian unit."

Courtesy of the 1 Canadian Parachute Battalion Association Archives.

Courtesy of the 1 Canadian Parachute Battalion Association Archives.

Members of "B" Company, 4 Platoon, 2 Section somewhere in Germany, wearing their official dress once again. As the paratroopers pushed further into Germany their dress tended to change. From the initial drop on 24 March to its arrival in Wismar, 2 May 1945, the Battalion had been deployed and on the move for 39 days. During the "race" to Wismar, the Battalion's rate of advance was so rapid that the supply columns could not keep up. Airborne ingenuity and initiative kicked in. Whenever possible, the paratroopers commandeered abandoned German vehicles, motorcycles, and items of dress. Paratroopers could be seen wearing German padded and sheep-skin winter jackets, as well as belts from which hung various types of German pistols. Occasionally, a paratrooper was seen carrying an M.P 40 Schmeisser machine pistol. Everything that could accelerate the advance, provide warmth and comfort, and augment firepower was taken and utilized.

Courtesy of the 1 Canadian Parachute Battalion Association Archives.

Members of the Battalion, in impeccable dress, form up on 11 May 1945, for a parade in Wismar. As of 7 May, Lieutenant-Colonel Fraser Eadie issued a series of orders directing that all German vehicles, equipment, and weapons had to be turned in. Inspections were routinely carried out to ensure that all Battalion members adhered to the prescribed dress regulations. On 16 May, the Battalion received 3 Parachute Brigade Administrative Order No. 89, which reiterated that all German vehicles were to be turned in. However, it allowed for such items as watches, cameras, shotguns, wireless radios, and binoculars to be brought back to the UK with the CO's discretion, provided they were retained as unit property. All enemy pistols were to be surrendered so that they could be dumped at sea.

"End of the Road — Victory in Europe." Members of 1 Canadian Parachute Battalion prepare to return to England to await repatriation. On 19 May, the paratroopers and their personal equipment were loaded onto trucks and transported to a local airport. Battalion members emplaned in C-47 aircraft and were flown to Brussels. There, some paratroopers were transferred to British bombers and transports returning to England. But when the bombers landed at various British airports throughout the country, they caused an administrative nightmare. Transportation was now required to return the paratroopers to their quarters at Carter Barracks.

Major Richard Hilborn was with the last group that left Brussels. "On the way back," he recounted, "I went and sat in the rear gunner's turret for awhile. It was awfully lonely out there." While lost in his isolation, the pilot warned him that he was about to have some fun with the unsuspecting paratroopers sleeping on the floor near the cockpit. The pilot "took this great bomber," Hilborn stated, "turned it on its side and did a dive and a turn, rolling my soldiers all over the place! He alerted me that he was going to do this. I was prepared and enjoyed the event while hanging on tight." Hilborn's plane landed 20 miles from Carter Barracks and, 24 hours later, all Battalion personnel had reported in.

Courtesy of the 1 Canadian Parachute Battalion Association Archives.

Courtesy of the 1 Canadian Parachute Battalion Association Archives.

Courtesy of the 1 Canadian Parachute Battalion Association Archives.

All photos: Courtesy of the 1 Canadian Parachute Battalion Association Archives.

Upon arrival to Carter Barracks, the paratroopers cleaned weapons and verified their kit. They were then granted a well-deserved four-day leave. Upon their return on 28 May, all personnel were busied packing Battalion stores in preparation for their redeployment to Canada on the evening of 31 May.

Fate was evidently smiling on the Battalion once more as space was found on a ship returning to Canada for the entire unit. On 31 May, General Bols, Brigadier Hill and numerous other British airborne officers were on hand to bid farewell to the members of 1 Canadian Parachute Battalion. The unit War Diary described the last moments:

"They had decorated Bulford siding with flags and bunting," it recorded, "and had a band standing by to play us away. A large parachute badge and a large gold maple leaf were made up on plywood, and added a distinctive touch to the decorations.... But in everyone's mind, as we left Bulford, was the thought that many who had joined us, were being left behind, in English fields, in the Ranville Cemetery in Normandy, in other cemeteries in Belgium and Holland, and latterly, on the Dropping Zone and in other places scattered through Northwest Germany."

After a short leave, Brigadier Hill returned to an unusually quite Carter Barracks. He missed his Canadian paratroopers, and on the 7 June 1945, Hill wrote a letter to former subordinate Lieutenant-Colonel Fraser Eadie. "It was very sad to return to Bulford last night," Hill confessed, "after two happy years we have all spent together in the 3rd Brigade, to find that the last member of the 1st Canadian Parachute Battalion had left.... The magnificent bearing and high standard achieved by all ranks of the two battalions (1 Canadian Parachute Battalion and 1 Canadian Parachute Training Battalion) will long be remembered by all in this country who had the good fortune to come in contact with, or serve alongside them. I shall forever remember, with great pride, that I had the honour to have under my command, both in and out of battle, a Canadian Battalion which is regarded by all of us as as fine a fighting unit as has ever left these shores."

Courtesy of the 1 Canadian Parachute Battalion Association Archives.

The men of 1 Canadian Parachute Battalion had served efficiently under the command of Brigadier S. James L. Hill. He would later write: "They won the respect of their British comrades and the hearts of many, and how proud we were to have them in our midst. They are now an integral part of that great Airborne Brotherhood formed in the War whose friendship transcends all borders of the Commonwealth."

Pictured are (left to right) Major-General Eric Bols, CSM George Green, Brigadier James Hill and Lieutant-Colonel Fraser Eadie.

The *Isle de France* returning the paratroopers to Canada. This 43,000-ton former French luxury liner, carrying over 8,000 soldiers and airmen, arrived in Halifax on 20 June 1945. It docked the next day at 1000 hours at Pier 21, Halifax Harbour. *Globe and Mail* reporter Trent Frayne described the atmosphere as the Battalion paraded in the streets of Halifax:

Courtesy of the 1 Canadian Parachute Battalion Association Archives.

"Only the parachutists were permitted to leave the ship, and they were returned immediately after their 75 minutes parade.... Marching six abreast the airborne troops were headed by their Commanding Officer, Lieutenant-Colonel Fraser Eadie.... The four-mile parade route was packed six deep with cheering citizens as 690-odd fighting men marched by, razor-sharp in their maroon berets, ankle-high boots that gleamed like polished mahogany, and khaki battle dress with the white parachute wings on the left side of the tunic. As they marched, the paratroopers received thunderous ovations from crowds of cheering people. The mayor of Halifax presented Lieutenant-Colonel Eadie with the Key to the City and the flag of Nova Scotia. Then welcome messages from Prime Minister King and Defence Minister McNaughton were read to the paratroopers. The following day the Battalion proceeded to a series of awaiting trains and left for a 30-day disembarkation leave to their respective Military Districts."

PRIME MINISTER'S WELCOME

During the Battalion's brief sojourn in Halifax, Adjutant General, Major-General A.E. Walford read a message of welcome from the Prime Minister, W.L. Mackenzie King. Walford passed on the Prime Minister's words while the unit paraded at Citadel Hill:

To the officers and men of the First Parachute Battalion: The Government and people of Canada welcome you on your triumphant return to your homeland. All Canada is proud of the magnificent record of the First Parachute Battalion. And, because your homes are in all parts of the country, the honour you have brought to Canada is shared by all the provinces. Although Canada's airborne troops were not a part of the First Canadian Army but were attached to British formations, the people at home are well aware of the vital contribution you made to victory. The operations in which the Canadian Parachute Battalion so greatly distinguished itself, the landings in Normandy and the crossing of the Rhine were the two most decisive military operations in the defeat of Nazi Germany in the West. The successful establishment of the bridgehead in Normandy and the equally successful crossing of the Rhine were the most intricate and difficult operations in which our troops participated. They will serve as models of such military exploits. From the glowing accounts we have received from the senior British officers commanding formations of which your battalion formed a part, we know how valiantly and how skillfully you carried out the tasks assigned to you. I am voicing the sentiments of the whole of Canada when I pay the highest tribute to those of your comrades who gave their lives on the field of battle and offer the warmest of welcome to all of you who have been spared to share in the rejoicing at the victory you did so much to win.

Corporal Gauthier is reunited with his family, 20 June 1945.

Courtesy of the 1 Canadian Parachute Battalion Association Archives.

Courtesy of the 1 Canadian Parachute Battalion Association Archives.

In stark contrast to the parade in Halifax, the welcome-home ceremonies in Toronto on 23 June 1945 quickly turned into pandemonium. "[T]he paratroopers tried to look serious and well-disciplined," wrote a *Globe and Mail* reporter, "but most of this had gone by the board when mobs of relatives and well-wishers and just people broke into their ranks on the street, and no one particularly cared." Mayor Saunders told the assembled men in City Hall Square, "history would record their great deeds of valor." During the speech a "paratrooper in the front row grinned up hazily happy, through a smear of lipstick. Another just held hands and looked at his wife and didn't care who said what, if he knew where he was at the moment. A big heavy-set fellow in the rear rank turned away from it all and stepped back for a moment to hold the hand of a pretty girl who kept looking at him without saying anything. Another ducked out, picked up a little boy, and swung him into the air. Spit and polish took a holiday Saturday when the paratroopers came home."

MESSAGE FROM THE MINISTER OF NATIONAL DEFENCE ON THE OCCASION OF THE BATTALION'S HOMECOMING

The Adjutant General, Major-General A.E. Walford also used the gathering of Battalion on Citadel Hill to forward a message from the Minister of National Defence, J.L. Ralston. It stated:

On behalf of the Canadian Army particularly, I add my words to those of the Prime Minister to welcome you home to Canada. You have fulfilled every task entrusted to you. You have made a great contribution to the victory over Germany and we are indeed all very proud of the valour of the skill at arms and of the effectiveness with which you have carried through your operations in battle. We are very proud too of the high reputation of discipline, which you have established for yourselves. I am very pleased to know that so many of you have volunteered to carry on the fight against our one remaining enemy in the Far East.

PART VI

POSTSCRIPT

Following their 30-day leave most of the Battalion members returned to Camp Niagara-on-the Lake, Ontario. Rumours were circulating that some Battalion members would be given the opportunity to work with an American unit that would be deployed in the Pacific Theatre. Meanwhile, Battalion personnel spent the last week in July setting up a tent city complete with floor boards and electricity. No one knew where the Battalion stores and weapons were. Training was at a minimum; nonetheless, every effort was made to keep personnel occupied. Many took part in organized sports and Lieutenant Robert Firlotte ran a boxing clinic. Others preferred to earn extra money and worked as fruit pickers in the Niagara Peninsula. On 8 August, over one hundred Battalion members went to Toronto and formed an Honour Guard during the awards ceremony for Corporal F.C. Topham, at which time he formally received his Victoria Cross. By mid-August, Battalion personnel were sent in groups to their respective Military Districts for final release.

On 22 September a muster parade was held at which time Battalion members were informed that the unit would be disbanded and brought to nil strength. As of 27 September, all that remained was a 42-member rear-guard party. The unit's administrative records were packed and delivered to the orderly room of the Records Branch in Toronto. By the 30 September 1945, the unit had been brought to nil strength.

For many, the soldier's pay book became more than just a record of their service and accomplishments. It was also a reminder of friends made and lost, and in many respects embodied the paradoxical cliché: they were the best of times and they were the worst of times.

Despite the disbandment of 1 Canadian Parachute Battalion, NDHQ decided nevertheless to retain a limited airborne capability formed largely by the battle-hardened veterans of 1 Canadian Parachute Battalion and the A-35 CPTC instructors. With little official direction, this small cadre studied American and British post-war airborne, airportability and air-transportability developments to ensure that Canada retained expertise in airborne operations.

Courtesy of the 1 Canadian Parachute Battalion Association Archives.

Even with a limited Canadian post-war parachute capacity, the professionalism of the Battalion's veterans, such as Lance-Corporal "Shorty" Hoskins, was instrumental in contributing and maintaining the hard earned lessons and experience of airborne operations.

Robert Firlotte, now with the Joint Air School in Rivers, Manitoba, was the Commanding Officer for a 60-man detachment comprising 1 Canadian Parachute Battalion veterans. These men ensured the maintenance of a parachute capability within the Canadian Army. Visiting Field Marshal Bernard Montgomery inspected the group in front of Union Station in Toronto on 2 September 1946. During that weekend the paratroopers took part in two demonstration jumps in front of over 50,000 spectators during the International Air Show held at the De Havilland Airport. The three aircraft flew in over the DZ in line astern and dropped the paratroopers at 600, 700, and 800 feet with all three sticks in the air at one time in three layers.

Courtesy of the 1 Canadian Parachute Battalion Association Archives.

The first formal presentation of the Jeff Nicklin Memorial
Trophy to Bob Sanburg of the Winnipeg Blue Bombers in the
fall of 1947 by Mrs. Eva Nicklin, Jeff's mother, and
Lieutenant-Colonel Fraser Eadie.

Presentation of the Battalion colours. The ceremony, long overdue, was conducted by members of 1 Canadian Parachute Battalion Association, 6 June 1974, in Ranville, France. The ceremonies were presided over by General (Retired) Sir Richard Gale, GCB, KBE, DSO, MC. Also present at this ceremony was a contingent of the Canadian Airborne Regiment.

Courtesy of the 1 Canadian Parachute Battalion Association Archives.

The Major D.H. Proctor Memorial Cairn, Proctor Field, CFB Shilo, Manitoba, Canada, dedicated 7 September 1971.

Unit Memorial Cairn, Le Mesnil/Bavent Crossroads, Normandy, France. Dedicated 5 June 1982.

Courtesy of the 1 Canadian Parachute Battalion Association Archives.

Courtesy of the 1 Canadian Parachute Battalion Association Archives.

Unit Marker, Airborne Historical Walk, Fort Benning, Georgia, U.S.A. Dedicated 17 April 1986.

Courtesy of the 1 Canadian Parachute Battalion Association Archives.

1 Canadian Parachute Battalion/1 SSF Memorial Cenotaph, Town of Wasaga Beach, Ontario, Canada. Dedicated 7 November 1993.

Unit monument at Gonneville-sur-mer, Normandy, France. Dedicated 8 May 1996.

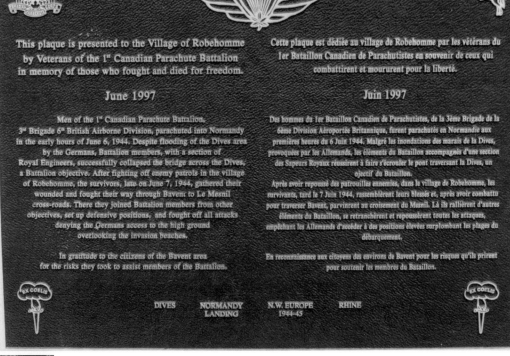

Commemorative unit memorial plaque presented to the Village of Robehomme, France. Dedicated 7 June 1997.

Courtesy of the 1 Canadian Parachute Battalion Association Archives.

Unit monument and plaque, Varaville, France. Dedicated 7 June 1997.

Courtesy of the 1 Canadian Parachute Battalion Association Archives.

The unit plaque commemorating 1 Canadian Parachute Battalion patrolling actions from 22 January and 21 February 1945, in Buggernum, Holland. Dedicated 9 May 1995.

Courtesy of the 1 Canadian Parachute Battalion Association Archives.

Unveiling of the unit plaque inside Garrison Church, Bulford, England. Dedicated 1 June 1997.

Courtesy of the 1 Canadian Parachute Battalion Association Archives.

Unit plaque (placed on existing monument), Varaville, France. Dedicated June 1997.

Unit plaque placed at the front entrance of the Rose and Crown Pub, Bulford, England. Dedicated 20 June 1998.

The unit memorial as part of Home Fires Park, CFB Petawawa, Ontario, Canada. Dedicated 8 July 2000.

The unit memorial at Ex Coelis Mountain,
Siffleur Falls Staging Area, Alberta, Canada.
Dedicated September 2000.

GLOSSARY

AFV	Armoured Fighting Vehicle
AGL	Above Ground Level
AROC	Airborne Research and Development Centre
BSP	Basic Security Plan
CATM	Canadian Army Training Memorandums
1 Cdn Para Bn	1st Canadian Parachute Battalion
Capt	Captain
CFB	Canadian Forces Base
CGS	Chief of the General Staff
CIBG	Canadian Infantry Brigade Group
CJATC	Canadian Joint Air Training Centre
CFPU CNL	Canadian Forces Photographic Unit Central Negative Library
CO	Commanding Officer
Coy	Company
CP	Command Post
Cpl	Corporal
CPTC	[A-35] Canadian Parachute Training Centre
CSM	Company Sergeant Major
CWAC	Canadian Women's Army Corps
DCO	Deputy Commanding Officer
DHH	Directorate of History and Heritage
DLO	Director of Land Operations
DMO & P	Director Military Operations and Plans
DMT	Directorate of Military Training
DND	Department of National Defence
DZ	Drop Zone
Ex	Exercise
FOO	Forward Observation Officer
FSSF	First Special Service Force
GOC	General Officer Commanding

HQ	Headquarters
IWM	Imperial War Museum
JAS	Joint Air School
JM	Jumpmaster
km	kilometre
LCol	Lieutenant-Colonel
Lt	Lieutenant
Maj	Major
MND	Minister of National Defence
MWO	Master Warrant Officer
NA	National Archives of Canada
NCO	Non-Commissioned Officer
NDHQ	National Defence Headquarters
NLC	National Library of Canada
NRMA	National Resources Mobilization Act
OC	Officer Commanding
Ops O	Operations Officer
OR	Other Ranks
P-Hour	Parachute Hour (time a drop will commence)
PJBD	Permanent Joint Board of Defence
Pl	Platoon
PMW	[A-35] Parachute Maintenance Wing
PW	Prisoner of War
PT	Physical Training
QM	Quarter Master
RAF	Royal Air Force
RCAF	Royal Canadian Air Force
RCE	Royal Canadian Engineers
RCIC	Royal Canadian Infantry Corps
RHQ	Regimental Headquarters
RM	Regimental Major
RQMS	Regimental Quarter Master Sergeant
RSM	Regimental Sergeant Major
Sect	Section
Sgt	Sergeant
SMG	Sub-machine gun (9mm)
VCGS	Vice Chief of the General Staff

BIBLIOGRAPHY —
ARTICLES AND BOOKS ON 1 CDN PARACHUTE BN

SELECTED BIBLIOGRAPHY

The following summary provides a synopsis of written material that has a substantial emphasis, or primary focus on, 1 Canadian Parachute Battalion:

Anderson, Boyd M. *Grass Roots*. Saskatchewan: Windspeak Press, Wood Mountain, 1996.

Anderson, James C. "Canada's Paratroopers Don't Have Stage Fright." *Saturday Night* 11,11 (December 12 1942): .

Anderson, R. F. "1st Canadian Parachute Battalion in the Ardennes: A Personal Account." *Canadian Military History* 8,4 (Autumn 1999): 5968.

Arthur, Max. *Men of the Red Beret*. London: Century Hutchinson Ltd., 1990.

"Canada's Jumping Jacks." *Khaki* (September 29 1943): 1, 4.

Canadian Airborne Regiment. "Founding Units of the Canadian Airborne Regiment: The First Canadian Parachute Battalion." *The Maroon Beret, Tenth Anniversary Journal: 1968 1978* (1978): 2.

Canadian Airborne Regiment. "1st Canadian Parachute Battalion." *The Maroon Beret, 20th Anniversary Issue* (1988): 1420.

Canadian Airborne Regiment. "1st Canadian Parachute Battalion." *The Maroon Beret, 25th Anniversary Issue*, 1993, 9-11.

Clark, Thomas and Harry Pugh. *Canadian Airborne Insignia 1942-Present.* Arlington: C&D Enterprises, 1994.

"Corporal Fredrick George Topham." *Pegasus* 1,2 (July 1946): 39.

Cottingham, Peter Layton. *Once Upon a Wartime: A Canadian Who Survived the Devil's Brigade.* Brandon, Manitoba, 1996.

Department of National Defence, Directorate of History and Heritage. "The 1st Canadian Parachute Battalion in the Low Countries and in Germany, Final Operations, (2 January - 18 February and 24 March - 5 May 1945)." Report No 17, Historical Section (G.S.), Army Headquarters, 27 October 1947, 36.

————. "The 1st Canadian Parachute Battalion in France, 6 June-6 September 1943." Report No 26, Historical Section (G.S.), Army Headquarters, 23 August 1949.

————. " The 1st Canadian Parachute Battalion Organization and Training, July 1942-June 1944." Report No 138, Historical Section (G.S.), Army Headquarters, 7 July 1945.

Flint, George. "Canadian Paratroop Training." *B.M.A. Blitz* 2,3 (March 1944): 25.

Gough, Larry. "Parachutists Want it Tough." *Liberty* 20,49 (December 4 1943): 89, 3739.

Harclerode, Peter. *Go To It! The Illustrated History of the 6th Airborne Division.* London: Caxton Editions, 2000.

Hartigan, Dan. *A Rising of Courage.* Calgary: Drop Zone Publishers, 2000.

————. "The Development of 1st Canadian Parachute Battalion." *esprit de corps* 2,1: 3032.

————. *The Importance of 1st Canadian Parachute Battalion's D-Day Objectives in Normandy.* Calgary: 1 Cdn Para Bn Assn Pamphlet, 1988.

————. *1st Canadian Parachute Battalion Assault on the Rhine: The Ride, The Drop and The Objectives*. Calgary: 1 Cdn Para Assn Pamphlet, 1989.

Hilborn, Richard. *It's Been Fun*. Private Printing, October 1998.

Horn, Bernd. *Bastard Sons: A Critical Examination of Canada's Airborne Experience, 1942-1995*. St. Catharines: Vanwell Publishing, 2001.

————. "No Challenge Too Daunting: Understanding the Airborne Mystique," *The Airborne Quarterly*, Summer 2000, 51-58; *Airborne Canada*, Summer 2000, 10-16; *The Maroon Beret*, Fall 2000, 43-47.

————. "The Canadian Airborne as a Military Elite: Fact or Fiction?" *Airborne Canada: The Journal of the Canadian Airborne Forces Association*, January 2000, 9-13; *Airborne Quarterly*, Fall 2000, 102-105; *The Maroon Beret*, 4,2, August 1999, 38-42.

————. "A Question of Relevance: The Establishment of a Canadian Parachute Capability, 1942-1945." *Canadian Military History* 8,4 (Autumn 1999): 27-38.

————. "The Airborne Mystique." *The Maroon Beret* 3,2 (August 1998): 57-62.

Horn, Bernd and Michel Wyczynski. *In Search of Pegasus: The Canadian Airborne Experience 1942-1999*. St. Catharines: Vanwell Publishing, 2000.

"Invasion Proves Strategic Value of Paratroops." *Saturday Night* 42,5 (June 24 1944):   .

Irvine, J. Clyde. "The Backstage Story of Canada's Parachute Troops." *Khaki* 4,4 (November 27 1944): 1.

Johnstone, Harold. "Johnny Kemp, DCM: His Story with the 1st Canadian Parachute Battalion." Unpublished private printing, September 2000.

Keith, Ronald A. "Sky Troops." *Maclean's* (August 1 1943): 18-20, 28.

———. "Invasion Pattern: Air-borne Troops Trained in Canada To Meet Needs of War's New Phase." *Canadian Aviation* (September 1943): 45-48, 78.

Leblanc, Donat. "Descendu du ciel." *J'ai veçu la guerre. Témoignages de soldats acadiens, 1939-1945.* Edited by Ronald Cormier. Moncton: Édition d'acadie, 1988: 75-83.

Low, Floyd. "Canadian Airborne Forces 1942-1978." Unpublished thesis. Victoria: University of Victoria, 1978.

Maxted, Stanley. "I Crossed the Rhine with the Glider Troops." *Maclean's* (May 15 1945): 52, 54, 55, 58.

Munro, Ross. *Gauntlet to Overlord.* Toronto: MacMillan Company of Canada Ltd., 1946.

National Archives of Canada, Record Group 24, Department of National Defence. Vol. 15, 298-15, 300, 1 Canadian Parachute Battalion, War Diary.

Nicholson, LCol G.W.L. "The First Canadian Parachute Battalion In Normandy." *Canadian Army Journal* 5,8 (November 1951): 30-43.

Nolan, Brian. *Airborne.* Toronto: Lester Publishing Ltd., 1995.

One Canadian Parachute Battalion Association. *1 Canadian Parachute Battalion Association Newsletter,* 1976-2001.

———. *1 CanPara 50th Anniversary Reunion.* Toronto: 1CanPara Association, 1992.

Otway, Lieutenant-Colonel T. B. H. *Airborne Forces.* London: The War Office, 1951.

Petitjean, Bernard and Jocelyn Garnier. "Canadian Paratroopers." *6 June 1944, Soldiers in Normandy.* Dorset BH, UK: Histoire et collection, 1994: 90-95.

———. "Les parachutistes canadiens." *Armes Militaria*. 59,60 (juillet 1990): 54-59.

"The Paratroops of the 6th Airborne Division." *The Fighting Forces*. 21,3 (August 1944): 144-146.

Peppard, Herb. *The LightHearted Soldier: A Canadian's Exploits with the Black Devils in WWII*. Halifax: Nimbus Publishing Ltd., 1994.

Portugal, Jean E. *We Were There. The Army. A Record for Canada. Volume #2 of 7*. Toronto: The Royal Canadian Military Institute, 1998.

Rice, Gary, H. *Paratrooper: The Story of the 1st Canadian Parachute Battalion's First Regimental Sergent-Major, Warrant Officer Class 1, Wendell James (Knobby) Clark*. Carleton Place, Ontario: GEHR Publishing of Mississippi Mills, 1999.

Shapiro, L.S.B. "I Dropped Alone, by Pte Alexandre as told to L. S. B. Shapiro." *Maclean's*, (August 1, 1944): 5, 6, 49.

Storey, Edward. "1st Canadian Parachute Battalion, 1942-1945, Parts 1-2," *Military Illustrated, Past and Present*, No. 48, May 1992, 18-24; No.49, June 1992, 14-17.

Strickland, Todd, "The 1st Canadian Parachute Battalion, A Brief History," *The Army Doctrine and Training Bulletin*, 3,1 (Spring 2000): 31-39.

Willes, John A. *Out of the Clouds*. Port Perry Printing Ltd., 1981.

Wyczynski, Michel. "On a Wing and a Prayer. "C" Company's 1 Cdn Para Bn, June 6, 1944 Mission." *The Airborne Quarterly*, 13,3 (Fall 2000): 20-26.

———. "Canada's First Parachute Instructor Cadre (Benning Group) August-September 1942, Fort Benning, Georgia, U.S.A." *The Airborne Quarterly*, 13,2 (Summer 2000): 94-100.

———. "Canadian War Museum's Airborne Beret Collection." *The Airborne Quarterly* 12,1 (Spring 1999): 90-99.

————. "The Maroon Beret: Our Beret, Parts 1-3." *The Maroon Beret/Le béret marron*, 2,2 (December 1997): 16-20; 3,1 (April 1998): 16-23; 3,3 (December 1998): 17-27; and *1st Canadian Parachute Battalion Association Newsletter*, 6,24 (November, 1998): 44-47; 6,25 (April 1999): 39-46; 6,26 (November 1999): 41-53; and *La Citadel*, XXXIV,5 (octobre 1998): 21-23.

ACKNOWLEDGMENTS

As with any research project of this magnitude, there is an inordinate debt owed to an innumerable number of individuals who contributed their expertise, memories, resources and time. Our sincere thanks are extended to all those who assisted, either directly or indirectly, to this book. Although it would be impossible to individually acknowledge everyone, the significant contributions of some, oblige us to make special mention of their efforts. In this regard, we wish to convey our sincere gratitude to: Jan and Joanne de Vries, Fraser Eadie, Ken Arril, Dan Hartigan, Darrel Harris, Bob Firlotte and Andy Anderson. We must also make special mention of the selfless efforts and enormous support of the staff of the National Archives of Canada, the National Library of Canada, the Canadian Airborne Forces Museum, the Canadian War Museum, and the Royal Military College of Canada. Finally, as always, the actual completion of this project was dependent on two special individuals, without whose constant support and understanding, we would not have been able to finish. As such, we wish to acknowledge our deepest gratitude to our wives, Kim and Suzanne, who so patiently and tolerably not only suffer our quest, but continually provide the necessary encouragement. It is to them that we owe our largest debt for all that we accomplish.